# Student-Centered
# COACHING
## at the
## Secondary Level

*For Quinn and Eva*

# Student-Centered
# COACHING
## at the
# Secondary Level

## Diane Sweeney

CORWIN
A SAGE Company

**CORWIN**
A SAGE Company

FOR INFORMATION:

Corwin
A SAGE Company
2455 Teller Road
Thousand Oaks, California 91320
(800) 233-9936
www.corwin.com

SAGE Publications Ltd.
1 Oliver's Yard
55 City Road
London EC1Y 1SP
United Kingdom

SAGE Publications India Pvt. Ltd.
B 1/I 1 Mohan Cooperative Industrial Area
Mathura Road, New Delhi 110 044
India

SAGE Publications Asia-Pacific Pte. Ltd.
3 Church Street
#10-04 Samsung Hub
Singapore 049483

Printed in the United States of America

ISBN 978-1-4522-9948-8

Acquisitions Editor:  Dan Alpert
Associate Editor:  Kimberly Greenberg
Editorial Assistant:  Heidi Arndt
Production Editor:  Amy Schroller
Copy Editor:  Erin Livingston
Typesetter:  C&M Digitals (P) Ltd.
Proofreader:  Victoria Reed-Castro
Indexer:  Judy Hunt
Cover Designer:  Candice Harman
Permissions Editor:  Karen Ehrmann

This book is printed on acid-free paper.

SUSTAINABLE FORESTRY INITIATIVE
Certified Chain of Custody
Promoting Sustainable Forestry
www.sfiprogram.org
SFI-01268
SFI label applies to text stock

13 14 15 16 17 10 9 8 7 6 5 4 3 2 1

# Contents

# Acknowledgments

*Piglet sidled up to Pooh from behind. "Pooh?" he whispered.*

*"Yes, Piglet?"*

*"Nothing," said Piglet, taking Pooh's hand. "I just wanted to be sure of you."*

—A.A. Milne, *Winnie-the-Pooh*

Writers often say that they couldn't have written a book without the support of a long list of people. That's because books like this one are created through a series of conversations and insights with smart and supportive colleagues.

This time is a bit different. This time, I'd like to thank a single person—a person who has been instrumental in bringing this book to life. To the many others who helped me along the way, I hope you'll understand.

For over a decade, Mariah Dickson has generously shared her friendship, intellect, and passion for creating schools that meet the needs of each and every student. Our favorite pastime is ravenously discussing how to make schools better. My husband will attest to this and likes to point out that there is no lack of passion when it comes to our work.

This book is as much Mariah's book as it is mine (though she would never say so). When I set out to understand the secondary context, Mariah was my guide. When I suffered from paralyzing lack of confidence, Mariah boosted me up. When I wrote horribly convoluted drafts, Mariah read them and sent them back to me laden with insightful comments. When I felt lost in my ideas, Mariah reminded me why this book needed to be written.

As I crept closer to finishing the manuscript, Mariah began her own battle. After a devastating bicycle crash, she spent more than six weeks in the hospital fighting to regain her memory and language. The doctors made no promises, and we all held our breath that she would recover. And recover she did. While she still has some healing to do, she is well on her way.

I can understand just how Piglet feels when he says, "I just wanted to be sure of you." My gratitude is impossible to measure. This book wouldn't have happened without Mariah. Thank you for being my friend. Thank you for sharing your brilliance. And thank you for getting better.

## PUBLISHER'S ACKNOWLEDGMENTS

Corwin gratefully acknowledges the contributions of the following reviewers:

Leanna Brooks
Secondary Instructional Math Coach
Evergreen School District
Vancouver, WA

Tina Kuchinski
High School ELA Teacher
Gresham-Barlow School District
Gresham, OR

Deborah Mitchell
New Teacher Induction Coordinator
Merced Union High School District
Merced, CA

Linda Phillips
Teacher, Instructional Specialist—Mathematics
Evergreen Public Schools
Vancouver, WA

Leslie Standerfer
Principal
Estrella Foothills High School
Goodyear, AZ

# About the Author

 **Diane Sweeney** works with schools and districts in the areas of coaching, leadership, and literacy. The author of *Student-Centered Coaching: A Guide for K–8 Principals and Coaches* (Corwin, 2010) and *Learning Along the Way: Professional Development by and for Teachers* (Stenhouse, 2003), Diane holds a longstanding interest in how adult learning translates to learning in the classroom. In the past, she has served as a teacher and literacy coach in the Denver Public Schools, a trainer for literacy coaches with the Public Education and Business Coalition (PEBC), and an instructor at the University of Denver. Diane has a bachelor's degree in Education from the University of Denver and a master's degree in Bilingual and Multicultural Education from the University of Colorado, Boulder.

# Introduction

While *Student-Centered Coaching: A Guide for K–8 Principals and Coaches* (Corwin, 2010) focused on Grades K–8, this book will tackle coaching in middle and high schools. It is grounded in the same premise as the first book: that school-based coaching can be designed to directly impact student learning. When the focus is shifted from fixing teachers to collaborating with them in order to design instruction that targets student achievement, coaching becomes more respectful and results based.

I certainly hadn't planned to write another book in such short order. After all, I've been happily doing what I love, working alongside coaches and teachers in schools across the United States and abroad. It was during these conversations that I was informed about a lack of resources that are specific to the demands of coaching at the secondary level. Again and again I'd hear, "I like the idea of student-centered coaching, but it's different in middle and high schools. How do I make it happen in my own school?" Writing this book is my attempt to provide some answers to this important question.

## HOW DO I MAKE IT HAPPEN IN MY OWN SCHOOL?

I recently spent a week working with a team of K–12 learning coaches at International School Bangkok in Thailand. Miguel and Chris were technology coaches assigned to the middle and high school. They hoped to learn how coaching would fit into their daily work, especially since they had been hired as technology coordinators, rather than coaches. While my role was to help them employ a student-centered approach, they were unsure about how coaching cycles would make sense at their level.

In order to see student-centered coaching in action, Miguel recruited Matt, a middle school teacher who was using a new set of standards in his robotics elective. I would guide Miguel as he coached Matt through a challenge that was based on the rover that recently landed on Mars. Chris would observe the coaching as it happened.

We began by taking a close look at the standards for technological literacy, and decided to narrow our focus to helping the students understand the design cycle—that robotics is an iterative process in which the designer continually thinks, creates, builds, and evaluates. We developed the following learning targets (or "I can" statements) to anchor our work:

- I can break up the problem visually.
- I can develop and explain a step-by-step plan that includes equations, geometry, and measurement.
- I can work with a partner to develop my thinking.
- I can revise my plan to solve the problem.
- I can reflect on how to approach the problem differently based on what I learned.

Matt and Miguel had a relationship that was conducive to coaching. They clearly respected each other and were on the same page about the standards they were after. Their plan was for Matt to teach the lesson and Miguel would confer with the students as they worked in pairs to develop a plan for how they would move their robots across the surface of Mars.

When I arrived, Matt was beginning the lesson and Miguel prepared to confer with teams of students. Miguel rotated around the classroom and asked the students to explain their plan and how they were going about developing it. While he hoped to see the students breaking up the problem visually to develop a step-by-step plan (the first two learning targets), it quickly became apparent that the students had a different idea about what they were expected to do. Miguel observed that almost all of the groups were creating sketches with little attention to detail. He would bring this up when he and Matt talked later in the afternoon.

As they debriefed, Matt and Miguel agreed that the students needed a model for the type of planning they were expected to do. They designed a lesson to reteach the planning phase. To do so, Matt revisited an prior challenge to model how to create a plan. Then the students went back to their work and made detailed revisions to their original plans. By the end of the period, their plans met Matt and Miguel's expectations.

In a single day, we witnessed a dramatic shift in student performance. By framing the coaching around a clear set of learning targets and collecting relevant student evidence, the coach and teacher were able to respond to the students' needs within a matter of hours. This is what student-centered coaching is all about.

Even though they had been skeptical at first, Miguel and Chris now had a clear vision for how they could collaborate with teachers to move their students' learning forward. They even began to see how their role could stretch beyond classes like robotics, which are clearly associated with technology.

Next, we were off to work with Chris as he partnered with two high school teachers—a teacher of psychology and a teacher of literature. Together, we were figuring out how to make student-centered coaching happen in their school.

## HOW TO USE THIS BOOK

Much like in *Student-Centered Coaching: A Guide for K–8 Principals and Coaches*, this book includes a diverse collection of practices, tools, and anecdotes from a variety of schools. It features schools that are rural, urban, suburban, small, large, and somewhere in between.

To make the most out of this book, it is important to understand that it isn't meant to be implemented as a rigid program. Rather, the reader is encouraged to explore the concepts, theories, and practices in an open and thoughtful way. You will find more success by customizing the ideas and tools to make them work in your own setting.

It is my hope that this book will help coaches make the shift that Miguel and Chris have made. It is also my hope that school administrators and district leaders will read this book and understand how to make the most out of their own coaching program.

While the primary audiences for this book are coaches and school leaders, I hope you'll keep the students at the forefront of your mind as you read these pages. This book is really about designing a model for coaching that benefits them, as they are truly our most important audience.

*Goal: Enhance instructional practices*
*Increase student growth and achievement*

# 1 Student-Centered Coaching at the Secondary Level

This book is driven by a single question: How can we be certain that coaching improves student learning? A decade ago, when coaching was a new strategy for school improvement, very few people were asking how it impacted student learning. We made the assumption that if we improved instruction, then student learning would improve along with it. Our focus was on getting teachers to use what we considered to be effective instructional practices, and we assumed that if the teachers used these practices, then the students would learn. But now that coaching exists in so many of our schools, we have to be certain of its impact.

Student-centered coaching is about providing opportunities for a coach and teachers to work in partnership to (1) set specific targets for students that are rooted in the standards and (2) work collaboratively to ensure that the targets are met. It eliminates any guesswork or assumptions about the students' performance. We no longer have to cross our fingers and hope that student learning improves; we'll know for sure.

## WHAT IS STUDENT-CENTERED COACHING?

Student-centered coaching is central to moving students toward success, because it occupies the space between where they are and where they need to be (Figure 1.1). It is driven by standards and employs the use of

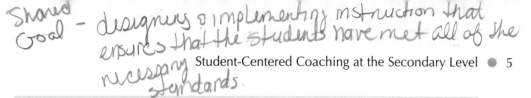

*Shared Goal – designing & implementing instruction that ensures that the students have met all of the necessary standards.*

**Figure 1.1** Student-Centered Coaching

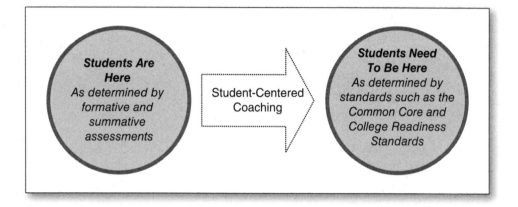

data—such as student work and assessments—to help teachers make informed decisions about their instruction.

Student-centered coaching is organized by a set of core practices that keep the conversation firmly rooted in student learning. As a result of these practices, teachers understand that the conversation is about their students and is not a judgment of whether or not they are doing a good job. Instead, the coach and teacher work as partners with the shared goal of designing and implementing instruction that ensures that the students have met all of the necessary standards—a timely objective with the introduction of the Common Core Standards in most states within the United States.

## CORE PRACTICES FOR STUDENT-CENTERED COACHING

- Conversations are framed by specific learning targets.
- Coaching involves regular analysis of student work.
- Coaching is driven by evidence of student learning.
- Collaboration may include co-planning and co-delivery of instruction.
- Coaching is ongoing and occurs with individuals and teams of teachers.
- Coaching is led by the school leader.

Student-centered coaching is a departure from coaching models that focus exclusively on the actions taken by the teacher or that make the assumption that if we improve teaching, then student learning will improve as well. There is some logic to these approaches, but an unintended outcome is that we've spent so much time thinking about what teachers *should* be doing that we've lost touch with whether or not the students are learning.

## A COMPARISON OF COACHING MODELS: STUDENT-CENTERED, TEACHER-CENTERED, AND RELATIONSHIP-DRIVEN COACHING

Most coaching programs are a combination of student-centered, teacher-centered, and relationship-driven coaching. While all three are under the umbrella of *coaching*, they maintain different foci and practices. They also get different results (Figure 1.2).

While student-centered coaching focuses on student performance, teacher-centered coaching is framed by the theory that if we develop the technical expertise of teachers, then student achievement will increase as well. The focus is on guiding teachers to use a specific program or set of instructional practices. It often blurs the lines between coach and evaluator, because the emphasis is on "getting people to do things," which often creates distrust and resistance among teachers.

Due to the fact that teacher-centered coaching focuses on helping teachers use specific programs and practices, this type of coaching may make sense in some cases: when a school is inducting a novice cohort of teachers, when a school is introducing a new curriculum or program, or in schools where the coach plays a greater role in teacher evaluation and accountability. Yet even in these situations, it is important to remember that the focus of a teacher-centered model is not student learning, so the impact on students may be secondary to the impact on teachers.

Relationship-driven coaching is less about holding teachers accountable and more about providing them with resources and support. It often feels safer, because the coach's role is about making the lives of teachers easier. And since coaches learn rather quickly that teacher resistance is par for the course, some may choose to back off and provide a more resource-based style of coaching. Though there is no doubt that this approach is helpful to teachers, it makes less of an impact on student learning.

The approach that a school takes often depends on its philosophy about how to improve teaching and learning. It may also depend on the school culture and the relationships that a coach has with teachers. It isn't uncommon for coaches to engage in all three types of coaching in a single school—or even in a single day. But one has to wonder: if we really want to ensure that our students are learning, doesn't it make sense to make coaching about them?

**Figure 1.2**   Student-Centered, Teacher-Centered, and Relationship-Driven Coachi

More Impact on Students ——————————————— Less Impact on Students

| | Student-Centered Coaching | Teacher-Centered Coaching | Relationship-Driven Coaching |
|---|---|---|---|
| Role | The coach partners with teachers to design learning that is based on a specific set of learning targets. | The coach moves teachers toward implementing a program or set of instructional practices. | The coach provides support and resources to teachers. |
| Focus | The focus is on using data and student work to analyze progress and then collaborate to make informed decisions about instruction that is differentiated and needs based. | The focus is on what the teacher is, or is not, doing and addressing it through coaching. | The focus is on providing support to teachers in a way that doesn't challenge or threaten them. |
| Use of Data | Formative assessment data and student work are used to determine how to design the instruction. Summative assessment data is used to assess progress toward mastery of the standards. | Summative assessment data is used to hold teachers accountable rather than as a tool for instructional decision making. | Data is rarely used in relationship-driven coaching. |
| Use of Materials | Textbooks, technology, and curricular programs are viewed as tools for moving student learning to the next level. | The use of textbooks, technology, and curricular programs is emphasized. | Sharing access and information to textbooks, technology, and curricular programs is the focus of coaching. |
| Perception of Coach | The coach is viewed as a partner who is there to support teachers in moving students toward mastery of the standards. | The coach is viewed as a person who is there to hold teachers accountable for a certain set of instructional practices or materials. | The coach is viewed as a friendly source of support who provides resources when needed. |
| Role of Relationships | Trusting, respectful, and collegial relationships are a necessary component for this type of coaching. | Trusting, respectful, and collegial relationships are a necessary component for this type of coaching. | Trusting, respectful, and collegial relationships are a necessary component for this type of coaching. |

## FORMATIVE ASSESSMENT: THE FOUNDATION
## FOR STUDENT-CENTERED COACHING

The idea of formative assessment as "assessment for learning" is nothing new. In the article, "Inside the Black Box," Black and Wiliam (1998) write, "we use the general term *assessment* to refer to all those activities undertaken by teachers—and by their students in assessing themselves—that provide information to be used as feedback to modify teaching and learning activities."

Many teachers have embraced the notion of formative assessment. They have more than enough grades to put in the grade book: exit slips, checks for understanding, graphic organizers, and writing prompts. So why are so many of our students still struggling? Isn't it true that if we are assessing *for* learning, then we are also making adjustments or modifying teaching and learning activities to move our students toward success?

It may be that teachers are overwhelmed by the demands of curriculum and assessment. With hundreds of students in several class periods a day, adjusting instruction based on the needs of the students can be a daunting task, especially since teachers often feel pinched for time, given the avalanche of curriculum that they feel they must cover. Decades ago, this very subject was tackled by Madeline Hunter, when she famously said,

> To say that you have taught when students haven't learned is to say you have sold when no one has bought. But how can you know that students have learned without spending hours correcting tests and papers? . . . Check students' understanding while you are teaching (not at 10 o'clock at night when you're correcting papers) so you don't move on with unlearned material that can accumulate like a snowball and eventually engulf the student in confusion and despair.

As Hunter suggests, if our goal is to graduate career- and college-ready students, then teachers need the knowledge, skills, and support to address the ever-so-persistent gap between what's taught and what's learned. We must support teachers in moving away from "teaching by mentioning it" (Wiggins & McTighe, 2005, p. 21) and toward teaching students to deeply connect with, and respond to, what they are learning. Learning is at the center of student-centered coaching.

## A CASE IN POINT: COREY AT BENTON HIGH SCHOOL

The hallways were crowded as the students at Benton High School found their way to their last class of the day. Corey was tucked away in his office, preparing for his first meeting with Jeff, an eleventh-grade social studies teacher.

When he was hired as an instructional coach, Corey's role shifted from high school social studies teacher to coaching across all subjects and grade levels. As a former social studies teacher, he recognized that Jeff had a firm grasp of the content and was passionate about teaching history. With this in mind, he organized their first conversation around nailing down the broader standards that Jeff wanted his students to master. Once they had the standards in mind, they could determine the learning targets.

As they got started, Corey asked, "What standards are you going to hit on in the next unit?"

Jeff pulled out the district curriculum and said, "Okay, so the next unit I'm working on is the Civil War. I could use some help with that. I need to teach the students the causes of the Civil War, they need to learn the major battles, and we also have to get at the reasons why the war began and ended. I have some activities in mind, but I'd love to pick your brain about resources and some lessons that I might teach."

As is often the case with teachers who are passionate about what they teach, Jeff's focus was more on the content he wanted to cover than on any particular standard. Corey worried that if they didn't focus on the standards, then the coaching wouldn't be student centered. He had been hoping to avoid taking a "coverage" approach, or as Wiggins and McTighe (2005) write, "an approach in which students march through a textbook, page by page in a valiant attempt to traverse all the factual material within a prescribed time" (p. 16), and decided to redirect things a bit.

He broached the subject by saying, "I agree that this is important information for the students to know, but if we refer to the Common Core Standards, we'll be able to see what is expected in terms of the reading that they will be doing to learn the content." He explained that since social studies was embedded in the reading standards of the Common Core Standards, they might be able to use both the standards and district curriculum to make sure that the students learn not only the content but also how to read and think in relationship to the content. He said, "Let's look at one of the standards as an example: 'Grade 11–12 students will evaluate various explanations for actions or events and determine which explanation best accords with textual evidence, acknowledging where the text leaves matters uncertain'" (National Governors Association Center for Best Practices, Council of Chief State School Officers, 2010, p. 61).

*(Continued)*

(Continued)

Jeff nodded. "I like that. They will have to get most of their information from texts, and this will help me make sure they think critically about what they read. If we focus on textual evidence, then we can hold the students accountable for what they are supposed to learn. That said, I still want to make sure that I cover what I'm supposed to cover—you know, based on the curriculum. . . ."

Corey nodded and said, "We can definitely check the district curriculum to make sure you are on track with the content, too."

As he headed back to his office, Corey realized that he had landed on a dual focus in his work with Jeff. Jeff would be able to tackle the content that he felt was important and at the same time, they would focus on how the students were thinking in relationship to the content. This would move them beyond a coverage-based approach and toward a mastery-based approach to instruction. He was glad that he had been able to push the conversation more toward the standards while also addressing the content that Jeff valued.

---

**Focus on Content**—the facts and other information that the students should learn; for example: what were the causes of the Civil War, what were the major battles, how did geography influence the war, and what were the factors that led to the end of the war?

**Focus on Standards and Skills**—how students read and interact with the content as is outlined by standards such as the Common Core Standards, ACT Standards, or College Readiness Standards.

## COACHING CYCLES AT THE SECONDARY LEVEL

Designing effective coaching programs at the secondary level presents a unique set of challenges. One of the most common challenges is finding a balance between in-depth work while also honoring teachers' busy professional lives. It is important to be flexible when it comes to scheduling, but there is also a need for coaching to be ongoing in order to make a measurable impact on the students and teachers.

I became aware of this challenge when I was hired to work with Corey's team to design, implement, and measure the impact of their K–12 coaching program. Their goal was to create a data-driven model of coaching that made a measurable difference for the students, and the coaches knew that they wouldn't accomplish this with "drive-by" coaching. So we introduced what we called _coaching cycles_.

We originally aimed for coaching cycles to last 6–9 weeks, with the coach spending 2–3 days a week in the classroom along with a weekly planning session. While this framework worked well in the elementary setting, the secondary team struggled to reach all of the teachers in their schools. Their schools were just too big, their schedule was too fragmented, and the needs were too vast. So we decided that a solution for the secondary coaches was to focus more of their time on coaching teams of teachers rather than individuals. They had the time, thanks to a structure that provided job-embedded professional development for teachers. By using this time to coach teams, they could make a broader impact across a school.

We also adjusted the length of the coaching cycles. We decided that if the following conditions existed, then it would make sense to decrease a coaching cycle to 3–4 weeks in length. If these conditions didn't exist, then teachers most likely needed a more traditional coaching cycle lasting approximately six weeks.

- If the focus of the coaching cycle is tight, clear, and measurable, then the students may reach the goal in a shorter period of time.
- If teachers are highly motivated and spare no time in applying the concepts and practices that are discussed, then it may make sense to decrease the length of the coaching cycle.
- If a coaching cycle is about refinement of existing practices and there is a strong foundation to build on, a coach and teacher may move through a coaching cycle more quickly.

We found that introducing a compressed model for coaching cycles allowed the team to make more of an impact across the large middle and high schools where they worked.

## Shifting to a Student-Centered Focus

Teachers often view coaching as being about them instead of about their students. Consequently, the first conversation in a coaching cycle often includes some redirection to establish a standards-based goal for the students. It can be helpful to think about a student-centered goal as beginning with "Students will . . ." and a teacher-centered goal with "Teacher will . . ." Goals for student learning tend to be content specific and are based on standards such as the Common Core Standards or ACT Standards. By comparison, goals for teacher learning are less specific and focus on pedagogical practice.

Focusing a coaching cycle on a goal for student learning doesn't exclude the coach and teacher from having conversations about effective teaching practice. There are plenty of opportunities throughout the coaching cycle to discuss pedagogy—the difference is that pedagogy is discussed within the context of what students need to know, rather than in isolation. By taking a student-centered approach, teachers are often more motivated to change what they do instructionally in the classroom, because it is framed around doing what's best for their students rather than introducing a laundry list of what they *should* be doing.

Figure 1.3 provides a comparison of goals for student and teacher learning. The goals for student learning are derived from the standards, while the goals for teacher learning are based on effective instructional practices.

**Figure 1.3** A Comparison of Goals for Student and Teacher Learning

| Goals for Student Learning | Goals for Teacher Learning |
| --- | --- |
| Students will use coordinates to prove simple geometric theorems algebraically. | Teachers will create a warm-up activity, or "do now," based on what the students need to learn about coordinates. This will streamline the time it takes students to transition at the beginning of class and get them involved in the math content right away. |
| Students will cite the textual evidence that most strongly supports an analysis of what the text says explicitly as well as inferences drawn from the text. | Teachers will use explicit modeling to demonstrate to students how to identify and cite evidence from the text. |
| Students will compare and contrast the information gained from experiments against the information gained from reading a text on the same topic. | Teachers will use a variety of organizational tools, or graphic organizers, to support students as they learn to compare and contrast information. |

## Analysis of Student Work and Assessment Data

Student work is the foundation of student-centered coaching because it provides teachers with relevant data about how their students are doing in relationship to the standards. In contrast, teacher-centered coaching is often about brainstorming and planning without a clear sense of where the students are at any given point in time. Teacher-centered coaching leaves the coach and teacher in a plan–teach–plan cycle that often involves little-to-no reflection on what the students actually learn as a result of the instruction that takes place. A student-centered approach creates systems and structures to carefully monitor student learning every step of the way.

In my early work as a coach, I believed that if the instruction was well designed and matched my thinking about best practice, then the students would most certainly learn. But that wasn't always the case. Even in class-rooms where the instruction looked perfect, there were kids falling through the cracks. I had to figure out how to make sure coaching was meeting the needs of *all* students.

I began using student work to guide my conversations with teachers. I found that anything that demonstrated whether or not students were reaching the standard was helpful. This included student writing samples, assignments, tests, interim assessments, exit slips, and even anecdotal data around student engagement. At first, the student work simply served as a tool to keep me focused. But I've found that when we use student work, the teacher and I are far more successful at addressing the students' needs through differentiated instruction.

In addition to student work, collecting student evidence during the class period is an invaluable role for the coach to play. By watching and noting what the students do in relationship to the learning targets, the teacher and coach can make informed decisions about instructional next steps.

Corey and Jeff's work followed a similar pattern. Having identified a goal for student learning, their next conversation involved unpacking the standard to identify a clear set of learning targets. Then they would be in the position to design and analyze the work that the students produced. They created the following criteria:

Students will

- read and comprehend history texts at an 11th grade level of text complexity,
- identify important events from the Civil War (refer to the district curriculum to identify the key events),
- evaluate the historical implications of each event using evidence from the text, and
- recognize when the historical implications are uncertain and back this up using evidence from the text.

## Collecting Baseline Data

Jeff had already given the students a pretest that focused on the facts, dates, and major events of the Civil War. But having reviewed the Common Core Standards, he and Corey understood that they must also assess whether the students could read and understand a text at an 11th grade level of complexity. The Common Core Standards state,

Being able to read complex text independently and proficiently is essential for high achievement in college and the workplace and important in numerous life tasks. Moreover, current trends suggest that if students cannot read challenging texts with understanding—if they have not developed the skill, concentration, and stamina to read such texts—they will read less in general. (National Governors Association Center for Best Practices, 2010, p. 4)

They created a straightforward assessment to use at the beginning of the unit. They kept it simple by asking the students to read a text and use a graphic organizer to demonstrate their thinking about key events, to provide textual evidence, and to identify important historical implications (Figure 1.4). With this information, Jeff and Corey were able to plan instruction that was based on where the students were in relation to the learning targets.

**Figure 1.4**   Graphic Organizer to Demonstrate Student Thinking in Relationship to the Content—An Example of a Student's Response on the Pre-Assessment

| Key Events | Textual Evidence |
|---|---|
| Robert E. Lee invaded Maryland and Pennsylvania during the Battle of Gettysburg. One of his main goals was to obtain food and supplies for his troops. | "General Lee's hungry Confederates crossed the Potomac River, the border between Virginia and Maryland, and marched into Pennsylvania. There they found food, supplies, and frightened civilians." |

***Overall Historical Implications***

The Confederate Army had diminished resources due to the battles being fought on the farmland in the south. Part of Robert E. Lee's strategy involved obtaining food and supplies for his troops.

When Jeff and Corey sat down to review the students' work, they found that many of the students clearly identified the key events that were featured in the text, but few were able to pull the information together and synthesize the overall historical implications. There was also a group of students who struggled to read and comprehend the text. This was alarming to Jeff and required that he and Corey figure out how to scaffold future texts for these learners. As a result of the assessment, they had what they needed to plan instruction that was targeted to the students' needs.

## Data-Driven Instructional Design

With the data in hand, Jeff and Corey designed the instruction that they would deliver over the next few weeks. First, they created a note-taking template that was similar to the graphic organizer they used for the pre-assessment. They decided to use the template for note taking as a vehicle for formative assessment. They also selected challenging and engaging texts for the students to read about the Civil War. Then, they planned how to teach the students to highlight and annotate the text in order to tease out the major events and textual evidence.

Since Jeff was a new teacher and not experienced in teaching reading, many of the instructional practices they discussed were unfamiliar to him. To help ease the transition, Corey decided to spend a few days each week in one of Jeff's tougher classes. During that time, he observed the students, took notes on what they were doing as learners, and co-taught some lessons with Jeff. They also met each week to look over the students' work and plan future instruction.

After four weeks, it was time to wrap up the coaching cycle. Due to Jeff's motivation and willingness to partner with Corey, they were able to accomplish their goals within a shorter amount of time. To capture the growth of Jeff's students, they reassessed the students using the same assessment that they had given at the beginning of the coaching cycle with a different text. That way, they were able to determine which of the students had reached the learning targets and which still needed additional support.

Jeff was pleased with how his students did in relationship to the learning targets. He admitted that when Corey first suggested it, he thought it would be challenging to blend the content of the Civil War with a standard that seemed to be more about reading. But as they engaged in the instructional design, Jeff realized that they blended quite well. His students gained greater depth of understanding about the content than he had expected, and he now understood that the students wouldn't only need the facts and dates from the Civil War to be college-ready—they'd need to read complex text to get there.

## LEADING THE COACHING EFFORT

Creating a culture of high expectations and thoughtful reflection is often the first step in leading a coaching effort. In schools where expectations are high, the demand for coaching is also high. But when the reverse is true—when little is expected from the students or teachers—coaches often find that they can't get teachers to engage in the process.

It would benefit us to refrain from thinking of coaching as a silver bullet; instead, it should be thought of as an important component within a system that is focused on ensuring the success of each and every student.

Coaching is one element within a system that includes the following essential components for moving teacher and student learning forward:

- A learning-oriented and collaborative school culture in which all members of the school community collaborate to engage in doing what's best for the students
- Leadership that is focused on, and holds teachers accountable for, moving all students toward mastery of the standards
- A data-driven assessment framework that tracks student learning and creates opportunities to modify instruction to meet the students' needs
- High-quality instruction that is differentiated and based on the required knowledge and skills
- Coaching that provides teachers with support to plan, teach, and assess students so that they will graduate career- and college-ready

In schools where the coach and school leader work in partnership, coaching becomes a vehicle for deep implementation, refined teaching practice, and most important, increased student learning. When principals have clear goals for student growth, they understand that the coach is an invaluable partner in the process.

A well-designed coaching effort also involves careful consideration of how teachers will be supported and held accountable for continuous improvement. It is the role of the school leader to set expectations and then hold the teachers accountable to deliver results. The coach, on the other hand, provides support so that everyone can get there. As Michael Fullan (2009) suggests, the principal and coach establish a seamless system of pressure and support that moves the learning forward: "The more that pressure and support become seamless, the more effective the change process will be at getting things to happen" (p. 17).

It takes a bit more than accountability to create a system that moves teacher and student learning forward. Establishing a learning-oriented school culture is paramount to leading a coaching effort. Roland Barth (2007) writes, "Schools exist to promote learning in all their inhabitants. Whether we are called teachers, principals, professors, or parents, our primary responsibility is to promote learning in others and in ourselves" (p. 163). Leaders who create a school climate that is based on trying new things, taking risks, and not settling for the status quo find coaching to be a great fit. But when these qualities are not in place, coaching often falls flat.

The most important message that a principal can send is that everyone is a candidate for coaching because everyone has students with needs. If the school leadership understands and communicates the rationale and practices that underpin student-centered coaching, then the teachers begin to understand that coaching is not about fixing teachers but instead is about working collaboratively to move the student learning forward.

The disappointing reality is that there are many examples of coaches who find it difficult to get leadership support, aren't being used to their full potential, and are frustrated and unsure of whether they are making an impact. Typically, these are your committed teacher-leaders who became coaches and then found that nobody really knows what to do with them.

Often this is the consequence of failing to adequately prepare principals to collaborate effectively with coaches. They know that they have to improve student achievement but aren't sure how to create conditions that support the coaching effort. Unfortunately, this is a common scenario that leads to an obvious waste of resources.

## TOOLS AND TECHNIQUES

Corey spent a fair amount of time observing Jeff and his students throughout the coaching cycle. He designed the following note-taking tool to gather information about how the students were acquiring content knowledge (Figure 1.5).

**Figure 1.5** Corey's Note-Taking Tool

| Learning Targets: <ul><li>Identify important events from the Civil War (refer to the district curriculum to identify the key events).</li><li>Evaluate the historical implications of each event using evidence from the text.</li><li>Recognize when the historical implications are uncertain, and back this up using evidence from the text.</li></ul> | |
| --- | --- |
| Evidence of Students' Mastery of the Content of the Civil War: | Evidence of Students' Mastery of the Common Core Standards: |
| | |

## Logs

..e following logs can be used with individuals, teams, or pairs of teachers. As is the case with any tool that is provided in this book, you are encouraged to adapt and adjust these logs to suit your needs (Figure 1.6).

**Figure 1.6** Student-Centered Coaching Logs

**Coaching Log: Identifying a Goal for Student Learning**

1. What is our goal for student learning for this coaching cycle? How does our goal connect with the standards?

2. What are the learning targets for this standard?

3. What are some options for assessing students in relationship to the learning targets?

4. When will we meet again and what are our next steps?

**Coaching Log: Creating a Plan for Assessment**

1. How will we assess the students to show growth across the coaching cycle? (Note: You can use an existing assessment or create your own.)

2. What is the timeline for collecting pre-assessment data?

3. When will we meet again to analyze the data that we collect?

**Coaching Log: Documenting Baseline Data**

1. Which students were assessed? Please attach a copy of the assessment used.

2. How many students performed at a proficient level, based on the baseline assessment?

   _____ % of students performed at _____ level as determined by the assessment.

3. Based on the data, what are our plans for instruction?

4. Does the data indicate any ways in which we should differentiate learning for students? If so, how?

5. When will we meet again and what are our next steps?

---

**Coaching Log: Delivering Instruction and Monitoring Student Learning**

1. How are the students progressing toward the learning targets? What is our evidence?

2. What are the next steps for instruction?

3. What should we do about students who aren't moving forward?

4. When will we meet again and what are our next steps?

---

**Coaching Log: Measuring Impact of the Coaching Cycle**

1. Which students were assessed? Please attach a copy of the assessment used.

2. As a result of the coaching cycle, how many of the students performed at a proficient level?

    _____ % of students performed at _____ level as determined by the assessment.

3. Does this data indicate any next steps for student learning?

4. What support does the teacher still need from the coach?

---

## IN SUMMARY

We are aspiring to accomplish something that has never been done before—preparing our students to be career- and college-ready, no matter what city, town, or background they come from. There are plenty of teachers who understand that they have to push against a system of seat time and credits and toward one of standards mastery, but they can't make this happen as individuals in isolated classrooms. It's just too hard.

Using the practices outlined in this chapter establishes a partnership between the teachers and coach. By having a clear goal for student learning and using student work to monitor progress and plan instruction, coaching doesn't have to be about making teachers do things that they don't want to do. Coaching can be about our students.

# 2 Getting Student-Centered Coaching Up and Running

**O**n the first day back from summer vacation, Cassandra moved out of her classroom and into an "office" (which most people would call a boiler room). She propped up photos of her husband and dog, visited with the teachers whom she was friendly with, and was wondering what to do next.

Just as the last school year was ending, Cassandra's principal approached her about becoming a full-time instructional coach. She was both honored and terrified by the request. She knew she loved teaching English and wasn't sure she wanted to give that up. But after thinking it over (and maybe against her better judgment), she decided that a new role would provide her with a fresh set of challenges and opportunities. She told the principal that she was willing to become a coach as long as she was provided with direction and support.

## WHERE TO BEGIN?

While it is fairly obvious what a teacher needs to do on the first few days of school—plan coursework and organize materials—coaching isn't quite as straightforward. Many coaches come into the job knowing very little about what they are expected to do on a daily basis. Cassandra could be counted as one of those coaches. She wasn't quite sure how to design her daily work, create a schedule, or even get teachers to sign on.

What she did know was that she would be expected to help teachers raise student achievement. How to get there wasn't so clear. She wondered if she should focus on the English department, since she was formerly an English teacher. Or maybe she could address content-area literacy by getting into classrooms in other subject areas. She decided that she'd better set up a meeting with the principal as soon as possible.

When they met, the principal warned her not to come on too strong and said, "You know what happened last year with the coach. . . ." Cassandra did know what happened last year: the coach alienated teachers by focusing on all that they were doing wrong. After a few months, the teachers began avoiding her like the plague. Cassandra didn't want to make that mistake, but at the same time, she did want to make a difference for the students and teachers in her school.

She asked if the principal was suggesting that she focus her work on the teachers who were interested, and the principal responded, "I wouldn't go that far; there are several teachers who really need your help, and I'd like you to work with them." Then she named a few of the most resistant teachers on staff as prime candidates for coaching. With that, she explained that she had to get to a meeting and they'd have to talk later. As Cassandra headed back to her "office," she wondered if it was too late to get her old teaching job back.

## INVITATIONAL VERSUS ASSIGNED COACHING

At the root of Cassandra's dilemma lies a question about whether coaching should be *invitational* or *assigned*. When I wrote the book, *Learning Along the Way* (Stenhouse, 2003), I advocated for an invitational approach and wrote, "We resisted the temptation to assign teachers to work with an instructional coach. This might seem counterintuitive or too indirect, but put yourself in the place of the assigned teacher and think about how you would feel if an instructional coach showed up in your classroom because you had been deemed a below-par teacher" (p. 46).

At the time, No Child Left Behind had just been adopted, and coaching was a brand new strategy for school improvement. Very few coaches knew how to create the conditions for systematic implementation of coaching and were left viewing it as a strategy for individuals rather than for a school community. Coaching was so new that they felt they had to tread lightly, lest they turn teachers against it entirely.

A lot has changed since then. Many schools have built a foundation for teacher collaboration through professional learning communities (PLCs), most states have adopted the Common Core Standards, and Response to

on (RTI) is pushing for a framework of improvement that is
nd designed to reach each and every learner.

nese changes in place, it has become easier to implement a
coaching model that reaches all teachers. Even so, I am regularly asked
whether principals should identify the teachers who will participate in
coaching. Coaches worry that they'll be assigned to "fix" resistant teachers, and principals worry that if coaches aren't assigned, then the teachers
who need it won't step up.

In order to work through the dilemma about whether coaching should
be invitational or assigned, I recommend asking an entirely different question. Rather than wondering *who* should participate, I recommend asking
*how* teachers will participate. After all, student-centered coaching is based
on the premise that every teacher has students with needs, so it makes
sense for every teacher to engage in the coaching effort.

As Cassandra navigated through this dilemma, she landed on this very
question. It seemed that coaching wasn't being viewed systemically in her
school. Instead, she was expected to work with the struggling teachers or
with those who would opt in. This was precisely what she had been hoping
to avoid. She didn't want to take a scattershot approach. She wanted her
work to actually mean something to the students and teachers in her school.

It seemed that she was on her own. She would have to figure out what to
focus on in her coaching and how to organize her schedule in a way that got
results. Since her school was knee-deep in the implementation of the Common
Core Standards, she decided that this might provide enough of a focus for now.
She didn't like the idea of sitting in her office and waiting for teachers to knock
on her door, so she created a variety of options for how teachers could get on
her schedule. She went after teams of teachers, since she knew that there
weren't enough hours in the day to provide individualized coaching to every
teacher on the staff. She also knew that there would be holdouts who still
wouldn't want coaching. She'd work with the principal on that, but for now,
she created the following options for teachers to engage in coaching:

- The coach helps teams to analyze data and plan instruction.
- The coach works with teams or individuals on an ongoing basis
  (coaching cycle).
- The coach meets informally with teachers to plan instruction.
- The coach observes in teachers' classrooms to provide student-
  specific feedback.

After getting approval from the principal, Cassandra shared her
plan and surveyed the teachers to find out how they would get involved.
Cassandra understood that she would be busy. But if she planned
carefully, she hoped to collaborate with most of the teachers in the

school at some point in the year. Her survey is included in the Too|
Techniques section of this chapter.

## THE FLOW OF COACHING

To create a sense of order around coaching, let's turn to the work of James
Flaherty and his book, *Coaching: Evoking Excellence in Others* (1999). Flaherty
introduces what he calls the *flow of coaching* or a framework that suggests
discrete stages for coaching. He recommends using the following stages as
buoys to mark how a coach progresses with each teacher (Figure 2.1).

**Figure 2.1**   Flaherty's Flow of Coaching

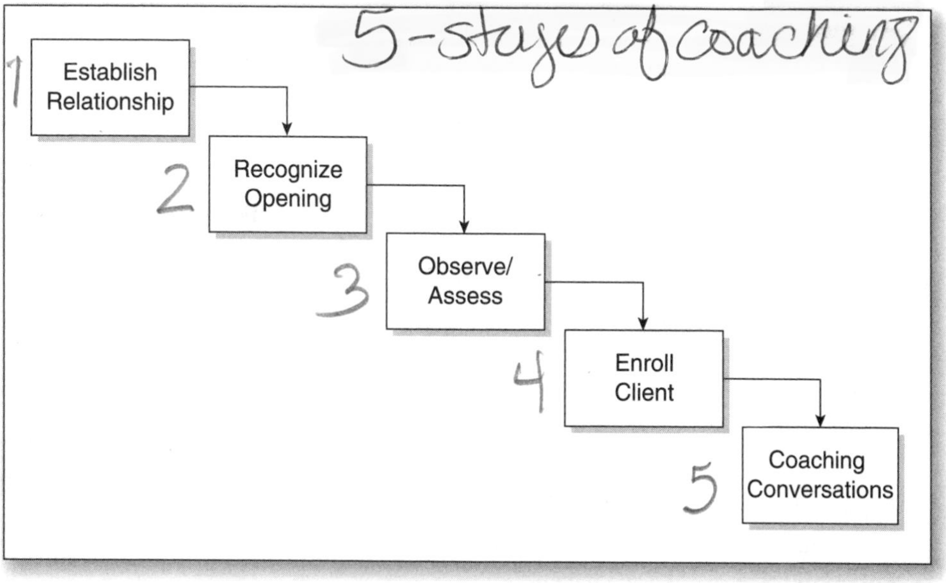

*Source:* Flaherty, J. 1999. *Coaching: Evoking Excellence in Others.* Boston, MA: Butterworth-Heinemann.

### Stage One: Establish Relationships

A friend once told me that coaching is like dancing with many different
partners. I love that metaphor and see it as applying particularly well to
the act of establishing relationships with a variety of teachers. Each relationship is unique. Each relationship creates opportunities for learning.
And each relationship can have its own challenges.

Whether you are coaching teams or individuals, creating respectful
relationships is nonnegotiable. Jim Knight (2007) describes learning as a
two-way endeavor and suggests that to make this happen, we must truly

believe that each and every person possesses the necessary knowledge, expertise, and skills. He writes, "In a partnership, all participants benefit from the success, learning, or experience of the others. All members are rewarded by what each individual contributes" (p. 50).

Creating partnerships across a school can take time. Coaches can't limit their coaching to those who they feel comfortable or friendly with. Instead, they must actively create coaching conversations with all teachers. Flaherty writes, "The type of relationship necessary for coaching is not one that's based upon 'chemistry.' It's more a matter of openness, communication, appreciation, fairness, and shared commitment" (p. 39).

Coaching also requires an incredible amount of poise and professionalism. As coaches, we have to resist the temptation to judge teachers. Instead, we must take a progress-minded approach that celebrates growth from both the students and teachers. Coaches who believe they know more than the teachers, are better trained, or care more about the students will always struggle to build relationships. And as Flaherty reminds us, "Relationship remains the beginning point of coaching and its foundation. Given that it's the foundation, it can cause the most problems when it is taken for granted" (p. 39).

While relationships are vital, it's important to keep in mind that they are not the goal of a coaching effort. We obviously can't neglect relationships, but we also have to move to the next stage in the flow of coaching if we want to get to the place where we can make a difference for the students.

---

### What It Looks Like

The coach builds a trusting, respectful, and collegial relationship to serve as the foundation for coaching. Relationships are developed through the following activities:

- Learning alongside teachers in large and small groups
- Collecting, managing, and sharing materials with teachers
- Supporting teachers with assessments
- Developing strategies for creating and sustaining the classroom community and student engagement
- Getting to know students and teachers by spending time in their classrooms
- Celebrating what teachers are accomplishing with their students

---

## Stage Two: Recognize Openings

In schools where there are clear expectations for teacher participation, coaches have little trouble recognizing openings. The fact that teachers *will* engage in coaching has been established, so all that is left is to identify *how* it might look. But as we all know, many schools can't boast a culture in which teachers understand that they are expected to participate in coaching as part of their professional growth. In these cases, coaches are left waiting in the wings and hoping that a few teachers will want to work with them.

A strategy for this stage is to carefully listen for openings from individuals or teams of teachers that trigger coaching conversations. Openings may come in the form of direct requests for coaching, challenges the teachers are having, or more subtle pleas for help. It may be that a teacher has been assigned to a new course or grade level. Perhaps there is a new initiative in the district that is requiring teachers to change things up. Or, as is often the case, teachers may be struggling with a challenging group of students.

I worked with a team of coaches in Midlothian, IL, and we started calling this stage "shooting the gap" after I shared a story from my childhood. My sister is six years older than me, and my brother is stuck right between us two girls. When I was ten, she got her driver's license and a cast-off baby blue Dodge Dart. With two working parents, it was her job to cart us back and forth to school, ballet, soccer practice, and piano lessons. We lived in Riverside, California, and would often drive up Central Avenue on our way home. Just as we neared our left turn onto Fairview Avenue, my brother and I would break into chants of "Shoot the gap! Shoot the gap!" My sister would veer through an opening in the median, spend a few seconds going the wrong way against oncoming traffic, and then safely cruise onto Fairview. We loved the heart-stopping excitement of doing something dangerous. We loved getting our responsible sister to break the rules. And we loved ending up safe and sound.

The coaches in Midlothian have found comfort in knowing that it can be a bit scary to shoot the gap. But Flaherty teaches us that when the timing is right, a coach can't hesitate.

---

### What It Looks Like

Openings for coaching come from the teacher and can be triggered in the following ways:

- A coach may hear what a teacher needs when participating with teams as they collaborate.
- A teacher may name an opening while participating in other learning.
- Data may present openings.
- A schoolwide focus for teacher learning may present openings.

*(Continued)*

(Continued)

- A coach may trigger openings by surveying teachers to learn more about their needs.
- Clearly articulating the coach's role may create an opening for coaching.

## Stage Three: Familiarize Yourself With the Classroom Context

While Flaherty calls this stage *observe/assess*, I find it easier for coaches to think of it as a stage in which you familiarize yourself with the classroom context. It's akin to doing an anthropological study of the habits of the teachers and students. I view this stage as an opportunity to identify what's working in the classroom and have found that going in with a positive mindset helps me continue to develop trusting and respectful relationships with teachers.

When I was a novice coach, I felt nervous entering the classrooms of other teachers. I didn't want to offend anyone or make them feel uncomfortable. I dreaded conversations like this:

Coach:    "Hi there; would it be okay for me to come into your classroom to observe today?"

Teacher:  "Uh, ok, I guess (looking nervous). Just let me know a good time. . . ."

But I've learned that after an opening has been established, it is quite natural to suggest spending time in a classroom, because both the coach and teacher know why the observation is occurring. It might sound more like this:

Teacher:  "Are you available for some coaching? I could really use some help with my 9th grade algebra class. They are having some behavior problems."

Coach:    "Of course; we can definitely set up some coaching conversations. But before we do that, how about if I spend a little time in your room to get the lay of the land? When would be the best time for me to come in?"

During these initial observations, I don't take extensive notes, because I never want the teacher to feel as if I am scribbling down all the things he or she is doing wrong. Instead, I come in ready to absorb my surroundings. Later, I craft a simple note to say thank you for hosting me. I usually include a few anecdotes of student learning that I observed so that the teacher understands that I am there to support student learning rather than to evaluate the teacher. I am always careful to remember what I saw the teacher doing well so I can build on it throughout our coaching conversations.

---

### What It Looks Like

As soon as a coach has an opening from a teacher, the coach learns more about the classroom environment by spending time during a relevant instructional period. This provides the coach with the ability to

- develop relationships with the students and build trust with the teacher,
- identify strengths of the teacher and needs of the students, and
- learn more about the teacher's practices in order to integrate into the classroom in a seamless fashion.

---

## Stage Four: Create Agreements With the Teacher

This stage is about setting clear norms and expectations concerning how the coach and teachers will collaborate. Some of the best work I've come across about creating agreements with teachers is in the book *Taking the Lead: New Roles for Teachers and School-Based Coaches.* Joellen Killion and Cindy Harrison (2006) write,

> Forming partnership agreements is a fundamental skill coaches depend on in their work almost daily. Like savvy, external consultants, coaches work closely with those whom they serve to identify their responsibilities, processes, and outcomes of their work. The intention is to create a degree of intimacy between the client and the coach that allows them to work together more openly and honestly. (p. 119)

The best time for these conversations is immediately following the initial observation in the classroom. At this time, the coach and teacher discuss the focus for the coaching, how they will collaborate, and how the coach can be sure to meet the teacher's needs. If I am working with a team of teachers, we have this conversation as a group. I like to use following questions to set agreements with both individuals and ms of teachers (Figure 2.2).

**Figure 2.2** Teacher and Coach Agreement

1. What do you hope students will learn as a result of our coaching work?

2. Is there any student work or data that will help us decide on a focus that would make the most impact on their learning?

3. In what ways would you like me to interact with you and your students when I am in the classroom (co-teach, model, observe)?

4. How often would you like feedback? How do you like your feedback—hot, medium, or cold?

5. I suggest a weekly planning session for 30–45 minutes; what time works for you?

6. It is also important for me to be in your classroom 1–2 times per week. What time is best for you, based on your goal for students?

7. How would you like to communicate between our planning sessions?

8. Do you have any other concerns or questions about coaching?

## What It Looks Like

At this stage, the coach and teacher develop a set of agreements for their work together. This discussion centers on topics such as

- establishing a shared focus for coaching,
- identifying the teacher's hopes and possible fears related to coaching, and
- setting agreements around scheduling and note taking.

## Coaching Conversations

When I was first introduced to Flaherty's stages, I was surprised by how much initial framing was required before we were ready for coaching. Now, it is easy to reflect back and see that I often skipped building a foundation with teachers and made assumptions about their needs, the quality of the classroom instruction, or how they wanted to collaborate with me. Using the flow of coaching helps me avoid these missteps.

① where are students in their learning?
② design & implement instruction that is differ.
③ modify instruction
    to ensure students meet the standards

Getting Student-Centered Coaching Up and Running

> ## What It Looks Like
>
> At this stage, the coach and teacher are ready to engage in the coaching work. Coaching can include
>
> - coaching cycles with teams,
> - coaching cycles with individuals,
> - working with PLCs and data teams, and
> - informal support to teachers.

## COACHING CYCLES

If the outcome of coaching is improved student learning, then coaching has to be in-depth and sustained over time. It requires a coach and teacher (or team of teachers) to determine where the students are in their learning, design and implement instruction that is differentiated, and modify the instruction to ensure that the students meet the standards. This takes time.

Coaching cycles provide a framework for designing ongoing and in-depth work with teachers. While coaching cycles have traditionally been viewed as taking place one-on-one with teachers, I have learned that in large secondary schools, coaching cycles are far more efficient when they occur with teams, such as by a common discipline or a common learning focus. Coaching cycles have the following characteristics:

- They involve in-depth work with a team, a pair, or an individual teacher.
- They focus on a goal for student learning that is driven by the standards.
- They last approximately 4–6 weeks, depending on the focus and teachers' level of experience.
- They include a weekly 30–45 minute planning session to analyze student work and design instruction.
- They include 1–2 times per week for the coach to be in the classroom to monitor student learning, observe the teacher, co-teach, or model instruction. Please note that when coaching teams, the coach may choose to rotate between the teachers' classrooms in order to monitor student learning and support the teachers when they plan instruction.

Whether I'm working with individual teachers or teams, the stages for a coaching cycle remain the same (Figure 2.3):

*Coaching Cycle*

**Figure 2.3**  Stages in a Coaching Cycle

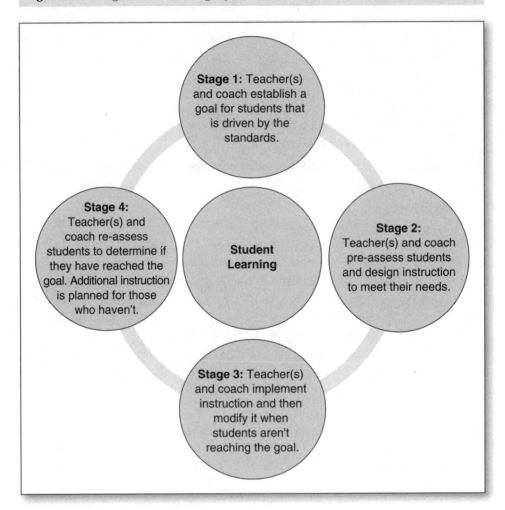

## What's My Role When I'm in Other People's Classrooms?

Coaches often wonder about their role during classroom instruction. Traditionally, coaches have either taught demonstration lessons or observed teachers to provide feedback about how they did. The thinking behind demonstration lessons was that if effective instruction was modeled, then the teacher would be able to perform the same techniques independently. The purpose behind observing teachers was to point out what they did well (or poorly) so they would (or wouldn't) do it again.

In a student-centered approach, coaches spend their time in classrooms gathering student evidence to identify how they are doing in

*This! Purpose of Student-centered coaching*

*perfect for science connection*

relation to the learning targets. When the targets are clearly established, the coach can productively look for student evidence in any grade level or content area. This approach is essential when the coach is working with teachers in unfamiliar subject areas. As a coach with a background in literacy, I have no business teaching a lesson in calculus. But with a clear set of learning targets, I can collect relevant student evidence to be referred to in future planning sessions.

## ENGAGING RELUCTANT TEACHERS

Risk and reluctance are first cousins. Since coaching shines a light on instructional practice and student learning, reluctant teachers will always be a reality for coaches. Roland Barth (2007) writes, "We educators will improve schools only when we take risks. It is as simple as that" (p. 215).

I find it helpful to remember that, at times, I've been a reluctant teacher who shied away from taking risks. In fact, I'd be willing to bet that we've all have been there at one time or another. As I reflect on why I've held back as a learner, I've noticed that reluctance occurs when

*why?*

- I believe that what I am being asked to do isn't in the best interest of my students,
- I lack confidence and choose to steer clear of new learning,
- I am fatigued by an endless churn of initiatives and reform efforts, or
- I don't feel that I have time to collaborate.

*curiosity*

One of the most challenging jobs of a coach is dealing with these all-too-real feelings among teachers. I've come to realize that one of the most powerful strategies for counteracting reluctance is curiosity. When coaches learn to accept teacher reluctance and to operate from a place of curiosity, they can begin to develop strategies to move past it.

*Curiosity* is about learning to think in questions rather than in answers, and it is in strict opposition to *certainty*. It is *certainty* that most often gets us into trouble. Stone, Patton, and Heen (2010) write in their book, *Difficult Conversations*, "Certainty locks us out of their story; curiosity let us in" (p. 37). It is easy to feel frustrated when teachers hold back, but it is our job to engage all teachers, even the reluctant ones. The following scenarios provide some strategies for doing just that (Figure 2.4).

**Figure 2.4** Strategies for Engaging All Teachers

| If . . . | Language You Might Hear | Then . . . |
|---|---|---|
| Teachers believe that what they are being asked to do isn't in the best interest of their students. | • "I'm so tired of people thinking they know what's best for *my* students."<br>• "I'd like to see *them* teach for a day!"<br>• "This goes against why I became a teacher in the first place!" | I never want to waste a teacher's time. I like to emphasize the fact that student-centered coaching is about the *students*. As I work to engage teachers, I find opportunities to share data from my other coaching cycles to demonstrate student growth across a coaching cycle.<br><br>I also work hard to treat teachers with respect so they understand that they are the primary decision maker in the classroom and that I'm not there to jam something down their throats. |
| Teachers lack confidence or know-how and choose to steer clear of new learning. | • "I'll let you know when I need your help."<br>• "I'm busy this quarter, maybe later in the year."<br>• "My plate is pretty full." | I work hard to build relationships with teachers during team meetings or other required professional development.<br><br>During these sessions, I learn as much as I can about each teacher and treat them with respect. It is my intent that the teachers who lack confidence will understand that they won't be put in a vulnerable place when they work with me. |
| Teachers are fatigued by an endless churn of initiatives and reform efforts. | • "If we wait long enough, the pendulum will swing right back."<br>• "I'm overwhelmed and can't make the time for this."<br>• "I feel that nothing I do matters anymore." | These statements put coaches in a precarious position because they are often viewed as being a "district person." This leads teachers to believe that coaches have a lot more power and influence than they actually have.<br><br>As a coach, I am always careful to stay above the fray. If I get sucked into these conversations or if teachers think I have something to do with district-level decision making, then my role is jeopardized.<br><br>Instead, I position myself as a person to support teachers in creating the best possible learning outcomes for their students. |

| If . . . | Language You Might Hear | Then . . . |
|---|---|---|
| Teachers don't feel that they have time for collaboration. | • "They took away some of my planning time, and now I have more students." <br>• "I don't have time for coaching." | While I work hard to ensure that I don't waste teachers' time, there are some who continue to resist any form of collaboration. As a coach, it isn't my job to tell teachers that they have to collaborate with me or their fellow teachers; this is the job of the school leader. <br><br>What I can do is design student-centered collaboration that makes a difference for their students. |

# SCHEDULING STUDENT-CENTERED COACHING

In her first year as a coach in a middle school, Margaret ran from meeting to meeting and tried to fit in some informal coaching conversations along the way. She felt like she was everywhere and nowhere at the same time. This lack of definition made her uncomfortable, because she didn't want her colleagues to view her as a slacker—not that anyone really questioned her work ethic, since Margaret was a coach and also taught pre-algebra and advisory. Now she was in her second year as a coach, and her goal was to create a more predictable (and sane) schedule.

At the direction of her principal, she focused her efforts on math and language arts for the first quarter. This decision was based on the fact that the language arts team had several brand-new teachers, and the math team was comfortable with Margaret, since she came from their ranks. She planned to create a new schedule for next quarter to extend her reach to more teachers the next time around.

This quarter, her schedule (Figure 2.5) included her own classes, time in other teachers' classrooms, planning time with the math and language arts teams, a weekly meeting with the principal, a weekly session in which she observed and provided feedback at a teacher's request, and a one-on-one coaching cycle with a new science teacher. She also had some time set aside for informal coaching and had the same amount of prep time as the other teachers in the school. While her schedule was rigorous, it was predictable and provided Margaret with the opportunity for sustained and ongoing work. She knew that if things got too crazy, she could scale back during the second quarter.

**Figure 2.5** Sample Coaching Schedule

| Margaret's Coaching Schedule for the First Quarter | | | | | |
|---|---|---|---|---|---|
| | Monday | Tuesday | Wednesday | Thursday | Friday |
| 7:30–8:00 | Advisory with 8th graders | | | | |
| 8:00–9:00 | Teach pre-algebra | | | | |
| 9:10–10:10 | Weekly meeting with coaches from across the district | In classrooms w/ math team: Joe's classroom | In classrooms w/ math team: Maria's classroom | In classrooms w/ math team: Susanna's classroom | Weekly meeting with the principal |
| 10:20–11:30 | | Observe Chelsea to provide feedback | 1:1 Coaching cycle w/ science team: Hank's classroom | Weekly planning w/ language arts team | 1:1 Coaching cycle w/ science team: Hank's classroom |
| 11:30–12:00 | Lunch | | | | |
| 12:10–1:00 | Open for informal coaching conversations | | | | |
| 1:10–2:00 | Weekly planning with math team | In classrooms w/ language arts team: Kathy's classroom | In classrooms w/ language arts team: Shelly's classroom | In classrooms w/ language arts team: Mike's classroom | In classrooms w/ language arts team: Dave's classroom |
| 2:10–3:00 | Prep for coaching and pre-algebra | | | | |
| 3:00–3:30 | After-school tutoring | Debrief with Chelsea | After-school tutoring | Planning meeting with Hank | After-school tutoring |

## Making Your Schedule Public

Teachers often wonder how coaches spend their time and can be suspicious of the flexibility that a coach has throughout the day. Rather than breed suspicion, I suggest that coaches display their schedule in a public place and send it out regularly to teachers. If, for some reason, the coach is gone for a meeting or training, it's important for teachers to be updated regarding when and why the coach will be out of the building. Sometimes coaches are uncomfortable listing names of teachers on their schedule, because they worry that the teachers may feel that being on the coach's schedule makes them look as if they aren't performing well in their job. My feeling is that if the school has defined coaching as student-centered, then this becomes a nonissue. After all, we all have goals around student learning; therefore it's something we all do.

## A CASE IN POINT: A FRAMEWORK FOR COACHING
## AT ARRUPE JESUIT HIGH SCHOOL

Arrupe Jesuit High School opened in Northwest Denver in 2003. It is one of 24 college-preparatory Jesuit High Schools within the Christo Rey Network. The student body includes an ethnically diverse group of approximately 340 students, with over 95% of the students qualifying for free or reduced lunch.

Arrupe Jesuit's mission is to prepare students for college success. Since the school opened, 100% of its graduates have been accepted to a two- or four-year institution. And when they get there, 72% graduate. Accomplishing this rate of acceptance and perseverance requires a continual process of reflection on how to best meet the students' needs—many of whom enter the school with gaps in their education and challenges in their home life.

The staff at Arrupe Jesuit has to know precisely where students are in relation to the college-readiness standards and then work strategically to ensure that the students successfully master them. They have made the commitment to graduate *every* student prepared, and they take that commitment seriously.

When the school first opened, Principal Michael O'Hagan quickly came to realize that he needed a person on deck who would work by his side to design a comprehensive system of support for the 20 teachers and 340 students in the school. He reached out to Brooke O'Drobinak, and she now serves as the Director of Curriculum and Instruction. Michael understands that even with a skilled coach on site, his role is to hold teachers accountable for meeting the needs of the students. He also understands that he can count on Brooke to help him make that happen.

### Focusing on the Students' Needs

Each year, the faculty tackles an area where the students are struggling to meet the standards. They select a focus based on teacher input and student data. Rather than telling the teachers what they *should* do better, Michael and Brooke solicit the thinking of the teachers so there is agreement about the most pressing needs among the students. As soon as a need is identified, the school addresses it through coaching and collaboration.

Over the past year, they tackled the topic of synthesizing learning—or making sure the students know when they don't understand the material and do something about it. This came from a shared concern from the teachers. They were finding that even with well-designed instruction, many of the students weren't able to complete their exit slips, summaries of learning, or writing assessments to the degree that the teachers thought they should. The exit slips simply weren't showing enough evidence of student learning. More than a few teachers came

*(Continued)*

(Continued)

to Brooke saying, "When I look at the exit slips, I wonder what I've been doing for the past sixty minutes! The students look busy, but they don't seem to be getting it." This shared concern created an opportunity for the faculty to come together to learn how to make sure that the students were learning what the teachers were working so hard to teach.

### Engaging in Collaborative Research and Planning

In the week before school begins each year, Brooke leads the teachers through several days of professional development in which they dive in to the research and plan around the identified focus for student learning. This includes reading and discussion, looking at data, showcasing use of technology, and exploring teaching practices to implement in the upcoming school year.

In their study of synthesis, they turned to the work of Cris Tovani and her book, *So What Do They Really Know?* (Stenhouse, 2011), and Eric Jensen's book, *Teaching With Poverty in Mind* (ASCD, 2009). Both of these resources provided insights and strategies for the teachers to consider, try, and reflect upon. By digging into the topic as a collective group, the teachers created a foundational level of understanding that sustained them throughout the school year.

### Creating Faculty Action Plans

At the end of their week of learning, the teachers created an individualized Faculty Action Plan in which they identified their goals for the upcoming school year. The Faculty Action Plan embedded their shared learning, reinforced the core practices of the school, included backward design and formative assessment, and was guided by the following questions (Figure 2.6).

**Figure 2.6** Guiding Questions for Faculty Action Plans

| Goals | What do you wish to accomplish this year? Consider the following: |
|---|---|
| | 1. curriculum design with emphasis on using backward design |
| | 2. instruction with improved mastery of core instructional practices |
| | 3. assessment that authentically measures student learning |
| Data | • What evidence or data are you using to determine your goals?<br>• What do you need help with to achieve your goals? |

| Progress | • How will you determine whether your goals have been met?<br>• What student work or data will you analyze? |
|---|---|
| Next Steps | • What will you do next?<br>• What do you need in terms of support and resources to accomplish your goals? |

While each teacher's plan was unique, they embedded the shared goal for the school year and provided Brooke with a blueprint for how to coach each and every teacher. She wasn't sitting on the sidelines, waiting for someone to request her support. Instead, the teachers had clear and specific goals that she could draw upon as a coach.

### Taking It Beyond a Catholic School in Denver

Brooke was the first one to admit that it was easier to serve the needs of teachers and students in a small school with a culture that was oriented around doing what was best for the students. However, the following strategies from Arrupe Jesuit can be applied in even our largest schools:

- School leaders work with teachers to identify a goal based on an area where the students need to improve as learners. Questions such as, *'What gaps are we seeing in what our students know and are able to do?'* drive the professional development. In smaller schools, the goal can be shared across a full faculty. In larger schools, the goal might be based on the work of a team or department.
- Professional development is designed to address a shared focus for improvement. This supports teachers in reaching the goals they have identified and also in moving student learning forward.
- Teachers create individual action plans to identify how they will reach the goal. These action plans are shared with the principal and coach and become a source of direction for coaching and professional development.
- The principal holds teachers accountable for meeting the needs of each and every student.

## TOOLS AND TECHNIQUES

How we get coaching up and running varies dramatically from school to school and depends on the school's vision, resources, culture, and leadership. As you create your own plan, it is helpful to remember that you may choose to adapt and personalize the tools in this chapter in order to best meet the needs of your own school.

**veys**

ssandra worked in a school that provided her with very little
ie decided that she'd better reach out to the teachers on her
ed the following survey to get the ball rolling (Figure 2.7).

**Figure 2.7** Cassandra's Fall Survey

Dear Teachers,

Many of you know me as an English teacher, but this year, I've taken the position of instructional coach. My role will be to work with you to identify goals for your students and help you make your goals a reality.

I am looking forward to working with you to implement the Common Core. To do so, I'm designing a variety of options for how you can participate in coaching. Please return the following survey with at least two areas checked. As soon as I hear from you, I will get in touch regarding our schedule and next steps.

___ My data team and I would like your help in analyzing data and planning instruction.

___ My team or I would like to work with you in a coaching cycle.*

___ I would like to meet informally to plan instruction.

___ I would like you to observe in my classroom and provide me with student-specific feedback.

*Coaching cycles have the following characteristics:

- They focus on a goal that you choose for student learning.
- They last approximately 4 weeks.
- They include a weekly 30–45 minute planning session to analyze student work and design instruction.
- They include 1–2 times per week for me to be in your classroom.

I look forward to working with each of you this year. Please return your survey to me by August 31st.

Sincerely,
Cassandra

## Monitoring Teachers Using the Flow of Coaching

I find the following matrix to be helpful for keeping track of where each and every teacher is in relationship to the flow of coaching. By making notes about where they are and what I plan to do next, I can carefully move each one through the stages and toward meaningful coaching conversations (Figure 2.8).

**Figure 2.8** Monitoring Teachers Using the Flow of Coaching

| Teacher Name | Subject/ Grade | Learning Focus | Stage on the Flow of Coaching | What Are Your Next Steps for This Teacher? |
|---|---|---|---|---|
| Jeff A. | 9th grade English | Student discourse | Stage 5: Coaching | Jeff and I are in a coaching cycle along with two of his teammates. |
| Sue S. | 11th and 12th grade math | Undetermined | Stage 1: Establish Relationships | Sue isn't sure about what I have to contribute since she teaches upper-level math. I plan to talk with her about ways we can collaborate. |
| Danielle Y. | Health (all grades) | Classroom management | Stage 2: Recognize Openings | Last week, Danielle shared that she is having some issues with classroom management. We are meeting next week to talk about options. After that, I hope to observe a few of her classes. |
| Scott P. | 9th and 10th grade history | Undetermined | Stage 1: Establish Relationships | Scott is a midyear hire. I will introduce myself to him and share my role and the ways that we can collaborate. I will also get to know him through his team's PLCs. |

## IN SUMMARY

The most powerful models are those in which coaching is perceived by teachers as how things are done. When this isn't the case, it will be interpreted as a weak process that isn't valued or required.

Without direction and leadership, coaches are limited to an invitational approach in which teachers are given the choice to opt in to coaching. Equally harmful is the practice of assigning failing or resistant teachers to be coached. This approach unfairly puts the coach in the position of fixing teachers, when what they really need is to be held accountable by the school administration.

Cassandra and Brooke's first days of the school year couldn't have been more different. While Cassandra received very little direction about how to design her work as a coach, Brooke worked within a system where coaching was embedded into the school culture.

While Cassandra created a collection of student-centered options for teachers, they were just that: options. She understood that without more direction from the school leadership, she would most likely work with pockets of teachers.

Due to the carefully designed framework for coaching and professional development at Arrupe Jesuit, Brooke was confident that she would impact all of the teachers and students in her school. One has to wonder if it makes sense to approach coaching in any other way.

# 3 Coaching Teachers to Assess and Deliver

The introduction of the Common Core Standards provides an unprecedented opportunity for coaching. In the past, coaches have had to navigate through a maze of content standards and expectations that weren't always consistent. But now, districts are focused on ensuring that a more cohesive set of standards is met by all students. The Common Core Standards provide an opening for coaching that didn't exist in the past.

The other day, I received a call from Marie, a reading coach in a Denver-area high school. She explained that several teachers in her school were worried about their students' failure rate. The teachers were in a panic, because the school administration was putting pressure on them to decrease the number of students who were failing their classes. Marie was in a panic, because she wasn't sure how to help them. She asked if I could come and observe how she coached Jim, a language arts teacher with whom she had a good relationship. She said, "I could really use some feedback."

I arrived the following week and met up with Marie in her office. When Jim joined us, I was immediately struck by his thoughtful disposition. I picked up on the fact that he truly cared about his students and wasn't sure how to move their learning forward. He explained that it was almost the end of the grading period, and he had several students who were failing his class. They had been reading *Of Mice and Men* by John Steinbeck, and many of his students either weren't motivated or weren't able to do the work. He had several struggling readers and felt that he had to spoon-feed them the book or they'd miss the point entirely.

Marie suggested that they look at some of his students' work to see how they were doing. Jim pulled out an assignment from the day before.

On it, the students had written down the attributes of the main characters in the book. As they paged through it, Marie asked, "What learning targets were you after with this assignment?"

Jim looked a bit sheepish, and said, "I actually didn't have a learning target in mind when I designed the assignment; it was just something that I thought would help the students understand the book." He went on to explain that he had spent a few days teaching about the two main characters, so he thought he should assess whether his students had understood what he had taught.

It was no wonder Jim was frustrated. He had been teaching to the whole class, creating assignments, putting grades in his grade book, and then moving on—a classic example of *deliver and assess* instruction. The good news was that he wasn't satisfied with this approach, given the fact that so many of his students were failing his class, and also that he had a coach like Marie, who would help him figure out how to solve the issue.

## WHAT DOES IT MEAN TO ASSESS AND DELIVER?

In *assess and deliver* classrooms, teachers have a clear understanding of what the students already know (through assessment) and what they should learn (based on the standards). Instruction is about bridging the gap. Teachers often find the need to differentiate learning based on the students' needs, because on any given day, in any given classroom, the students are in different places as learners. The curriculum goes from being *generic* to *specific*, because the teachers aren't guessing what students will need to learn. They know it because they assess the students first and then decide how to address the students' needs.

It really isn't a surprise that the reverse, or a *deliver and assess* model of instruction, is far more common in today's schools. Teachers are in a constant struggle to come to terms with what should be taught and to what depth it should be learned. In their quest to figure out what's essential, they have crammed in so much content that they have lost the ability to teach to deep levels of understanding. They have unintentionally created a model of delivering and assessing that prioritizes coverage of content over depth of learning. Students are awash in a sea of information that they must learn, and little is done to ensure that learning actually occurs. Here's an all-too-real example:

> It's April, just after spring break. You look at what is left to teach and the number of days left in the year and wonder how you got into this predicament again. If it's world history, twentieth-century study

may boil down to three quick wars. If it's math, geometry may be reduced to a few constructions or statistics and probability to a few games of chance. If it's language arts, poetry may get the boot. To avoid cramming large amounts of content into short periods of time, or "teaching by mentioning it" (Wiggins & McTighe, 2005, p. 21), teachers have to make hard choices regarding what to leave in and what to take out. (Stiggins, Arter, Chappuis, & Chappuis, 2006, p. 56)

Teachers don't like this system any more than the students do. In my coaching conversations, it doesn't take long to arrive at the matter of what to teach. I often find myself encouraging teachers to decrease the amount of content they teach, so they can ensure that the students learn what's been taught. This often doesn't go over well, because teachers see me as a challenge to their job stability, their subject matter, and their ability to cover what they think is important.

The adoption of the Common Core Standards is pushing states and school districts to identify what they consider to be essential learning for our students. The authors of the Common Core Standards write:

> The Common Core State Standards focus on core conceptual understandings and procedures starting in the early grades, thus enabling teachers to take the time needed to teach core concepts and procedures well—and to give students the opportunity to master them. (National Governors Association Center for Best Practices, Council of Chief State School Officers, 2010)

But adoption of the Common Core Standards isn't enough. If we are to succeed in tackling this problem, we will need to approach it at a system-wide level. We can't leave such a pervasive problem as a high failure rate up to individual coaches like Marie to solve. We'd be much better off building our school systems around the premise of teaching our students to standards-mastery levels in lieu of taking an approach that prioritizes coverage of massive amounts of content. Later in this chapter, you will be introduced to a school that is doing just that. But for now, let's look a bit deeper into the attributes of an assess and deliver model of instruction.

## A MARRIAGE BETWEEN BACKWARD DESIGN AND COACHING

Many educators are familiar with the concept of backward design in relation to curriculum planning. When I first learned about the planning process set forth by Wiggins and McTighe, I was immediately struck by its potential to inform my coaching. I took the following statement to heart:

> We are quick to say what things *we* like to teach, what activities *we* will do, and what kinds of resources *we* will use; but without clarifying the desired results of our teaching, how will we ever know whether our designs are appropriate or arbitrary? How will we distinguish merely interesting learning from *effective* teaching? (2005, p. 14)

When I first read this, I realized that I had to think differently as a coach. I had to build in more opportunities to help teachers become clear about their desired results. I had to figure out how to help teachers blend standards, differentiation, and a clear vision about outcomes in a way that ensured that students achieved the objectives we had set. It had to begin with the standards.

## Standard . . . What Standard?

Establishing an assess and deliver classroom depends on a clear vision for both the learning targets and the pedagogical practices that are necessary to get there. In the case of Marie and Jim, they started here.

While Jim wanted the students to be able to analyze aspects of the book, such as the characters and themes, Marie suggested that they look to the standards to create some learning targets that could easily be preassessed. She suggested that they start with the following standard:

> Students will determine a theme or central idea of a text and analyze in detail its development over the course of the text, including how it emerges and is shaped and refined by specific details; [students will also] provide an objective summary of the text. (National Governors Association Center for Best Practices, Council of Chief State School Officers, 2010, p. 38)

They agreed that there was a nice balance between the standard and what Jim wanted his students to learn. Marie suggested that they create a few learning targets to match the standard so that they could zero in on what the students already knew and what they needed to learn next (Figure 3.1).

As they created the targets, Jim realized that he needed to help his students create meaning from the book rather than doing it for them. They agreed that their first step might be to see how many students knew how

**Figure 3.1**   Learning Targets

- I can annotate across a text in order to track my thinking.
- I can identify how the central idea changes across the text.
- I can identify evidence to explain my thinking about the characters, plot, and themes.
- I can summarize the text in an objective manner.

to annotate text. As soon as Jim and Marie gathered this information, they'd be able to plan the instruction.

## Differentiating Instruction

A hallmark of an assess and deliver classroom is differentiation. There is no question that it isn't easy to deliver needs-based instruction when a teacher sees hundreds of students in any given day. But with coaching support, it can be done.

In the book *Integrating Differentiated Instruction and Understanding by Design,* Carol Anne Tomlinson and Jay McTighe (2006) write, "In teaching, it is necessary to proceed from considering where students begin the unit in relation to the desired results, then to implementing the teaching plan, and finally to gathering evidence of student success" (p. 155).

To make differentiation possible, teachers have to develop simple and manageable ways to monitor where the students are in relation to where they need to be. This might involve exit slips, conversations with students, listening in as small groups discuss their learning, jotting down thoughts on a post-it note, solving problems, or creating a graphic organizer. For their own sake, teachers have to keep it simple so that they can quickly analyze the student work and make real-time decisions about where to go next with their instruction.

Sorting sessions are a productive way to help teachers see—and act on—the different needs in their classrooms. In a sorting session, a teacher, or team of teachers, and the coach sit down with a pile of student work and sort that work against a clear set of learning targets.

I recently coached a team of middle school teachers as they engaged in a sorting session with a focus on drawing conclusions. The students had just completed a districtwide assessment that included reading a passage and answering some questions. With the student work and learning targets in hand, we were able to sort the assessments into piles that included groups identified as *exceeds*, *meets*, or *emerging*.

As the teachers went through the process, they began to notice some patterns. The most obvious was that many of the students understood how to cite evidence from the text. This was a relief to the teachers, because they had been focusing on this skill for several weeks. What most of the students hadn't done was provide enough of their *own* thinking about the text. It seemed that the students still weren't sure how to provide their own thinking, and without it, there weren't many conclusions being drawn.

Since this was an overarching need, the teachers decided to address it with the whole class. There were also some things that just a few students needed, so we discussed how to support those students while moving the rest toward the standard. Sorting the student work helped the teachers respond in real time to what the students needed in relationship to the learning targets. They weren't theorizing but instead were basing their instructional decisions on the student data.

## CREATING OPPORTUNITIES FOR STUDENTS TO SELF-EVALUATE AND RECEIVE FEEDBACK

Student self-evaluation and feedback are essential components of the assess and deliver classroom. The power of student self-evaluation and reflection can't be underestimated. In the book titled *Visible Learning: A Synthesis of Over 800 Meta-Analyses Relating to Achievement,* John Hattie (2009) identified self-evaluation as the highest-ranking practice for impacting student achievement, with an effect size of $d = 1.44$. Hattie wrote,

> An effect size of $d = 1.0$ indicates an increase of one standard deviation on the outcome of improving school achievement. A one standard deviation increase is typically associated with advancing children's achievement by two to three years. An effect size of 1.0 would mean that, on average, students receiving that treatment would exceed 84% of students not receiving that treatment. (pp. 7–8)

Furthermore, in *Classroom Instruction That Works, 2nd Edition* (2012), Marzano, Pickering, and Pollack identify "setting objectives and providing feedback" as the instructional strategy that has the highest potential to impact teaching and learning.

Working with teachers to create opportunities for the students to reflect on their learning and receive regular feedback is at the core of student-centered coaching. A team of coaches in Goshen County School District in southeast Wyoming have developed a set of tools to do just that.

Mike and Dewey were coaches who worked together at Southeast Junior High and High School. A primary focus of their work was helping teachers implement the Common Core Standards. After helping teams of teachers create learning targets (or "I can" statements), they realized that they might as well create opportunities for the students to self-evaluate, based on the same indicators. So they began working with teachers to create a success criteria to guide both the students and teachers through a process of self-evaluation and feedback (see p. 48, Figure 3.2).

*Example*

The following example is from a coaching cycle with Bruce, a math teacher of over 30 years. They worked with Bruce to establish clarity not only about what the students needed to learn but also about the purposes of providing the students with relevant and specific feedback.

As Bruce provided the instruction, both he and the students were quickly able to assess their progress through assignments such as solving problems or by using exit slips. The goal was for the students to self-assess at three different points during the unit. The last time was a few days before the summative assessment. By tracking their progress, there were no surprises when the students took the unit test. Bruce found that the students' self-evaluation was a powerful predictor for how they would do on the summative assessment. He and the coaches had created a method for the students to manage their own learning alongside him within an assess and deliver classroom.

## What About the Grade Book?

So often, the grade book creates a vortex that pulls teachers back to a deliver and assess approach. There's something about squeezing student performance into all of those little columns. Nobody likes it. And when grades come up in my coaching conversations (and they always do), I find myself asking teachers what forms of student evidence will best establish whether or not the students reached the learning target. Odds are, the student evidence isn't as neat and tidy as the columns in the grade book. We have to think differently about knowing what our students understand.

In Goshen County, Mike and Dewey were honest with teachers about the fact that they will have to exist in two worlds—the worlds of formative and summative assessment. They suggested that each time the students receive a check for understanding on the success criteria, the teacher would then assign a point value to it. They acknowledged that this can feel like it doesn't follow the true intention behind checking for understanding, but it allows the coaches and teacher to formatively assess and gather grades at the same time. Whatever we do, we have to make sure that our instruction and grading is driven by what the students know and are able to do in relation to the learning targets.

Success Criteria for Eighth-Grade Unit on Systems of Equations

| Standard MA8.F.1.1: Students will understand that a function is a rule that assigns to each input exactly one output. The graph of a function is the set of ordered pairs, consisting of an input and the corresponding output.<br><br>Students mark their progress on each skill in pen or pencil. Teacher will evaluate the progress with a colored mark. | Date | Information<br>I heard of it. | Knowledge<br>I can do this with help. | Know-How<br>I can do this on my own. | Mastery<br>I can teach someone else or apply the skill to a new situation. | *Evidence of Learning*<br>I mastered this because I was able to teach _____.<br><br>I did this on my own when I did _____. |
|---|---|---|---|---|---|---|
| I can identify solutions for single equations. | 3/6/11 | X | | | | I solved problems # 9–15; this demonstrates know-how. |
| | 3/9/11 | | X | | | |
| | 3/11/11 | | | X | | |
| I can identify methods of solving equations (graphing, substitution, and elimination). | | | | | | |
| | | | | | | |
| | | | | | | |
| I can recognize the number of solutions for a system and solve for *y*. | | | | | | |
| | | | | | | |
| | | | | | | |
| I can create linear equations with two variables. | | | | | | |
| | | | | | | |
| | | | | | | |
| I can solve a system from ordered pairs; I can graph two lines and find the intersect. | | | | | | |
| | | | | | | |
| | | | | | | |

| | | | | | | |
|---|---|---|---|---|---|---|
| I can read story problems and create two equations with two different data sets. | | | | | | |
| | | | | | | |
| | | | | | | |
| I can solve real-world and mathematical problems leading to two linear equations in two variables. | | | | | | |
| | | | | | | |
| | | | | | | |

## A CASE IN POINT: DSST PUBLIC SCHOOLS, DENVER

Denver School of Science and Technology (DSST) Public Schools is a network of middle and high schools that has figured out how to use the assess and deliver approach to get 100% of its graduates into college, with very few (>5%) needing remediation when they get there. It currently operates five open-enrollment charter schools that serve 1,500 students across Grades 6–12. When it reaches full capacity in 2020, it will have 10 schools that serve over 4,500 students. Figure 3.3 illustrates the student demographics at DSST.

**Figure 3.3** Student Demographics for DSST Public Schools

- 27.7% African American
- 42.6% Hispanic
- 20.2% Caucasian
- 5.3% Mixed Race or Other
- 3.8% Asian
- 53% of students qualify for free or reduced lunch.

DSST operates with an assess-and-deliver mindset. Its Instructional Data Cycle sets forth a clear process for teachers to assess their students through daily mastery checks, formative assessments, interim assessments, end-of-unit assessments,

*(Continued)*

(Continued)

and final exams. This provides the conditions for teachers to immediately analyze the data and then adapt instruction so that the students meet the standards. Teachers receive both coaching and leadership support so that they can assess, analyze, act, and reassess (Figure 3.4).

**Figure 3.4** DSST's Instructional Data Cycle

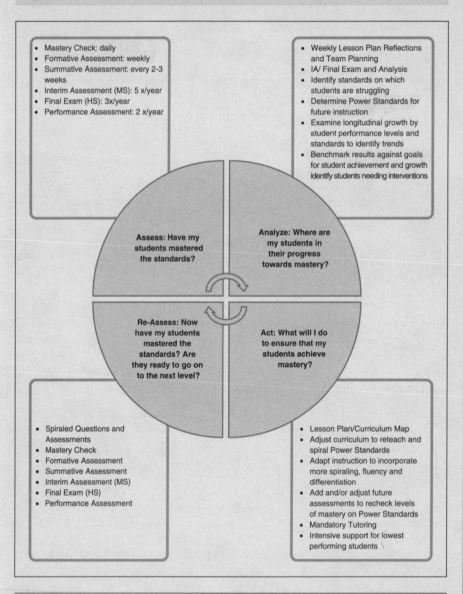

- Mastery Check: daily
- Formative Assessment: weekly
- Summative Assessment: every 2-3 weeks
- Interim Assessment (MS): 5 x/year
- Final Exam (HS): 3x/year
- Performance Assessment: 2 x/year

- Weekly Lesson Plan Reflections and Team Planning
- IA/ Final Exam and Analysis
- Identify standards on which students are struggling
- Determine Power Standards for future instruction
- Examine longitudinal growth by student performance levels and standards to identify trends
- Benchmark results against goals for student achievement and growth identify students needing interventions

**Assess:** Have my students mastered the standards?

**Analyze:** Where are my students in their progress towards mastery?

**Re-Assess:** Now have my students mastered the standards? Are they ready to go on to the next level?

**Act:** What will I do to ensure that my students achieve mastery?

- Spiraled Questions and Assessments
- Mastery Check
- Formative Assessment
- Summative Assessment
- Interim Assessment (MS)
- Final Exam (HS)
- Performance Assessment

- Lesson Plan/Curriculum Map
- Adjust curriculum to reteach and spiral Power Standards
- Adapt instruction to incorporate more spiraling, fluency and differentiation
- Add and/or adjust future assessments to recheck levels of mastery on Power Standards
- Mandatory Tutoring
- Intensive support for lowest performing students

## Clearly Articulated Standards

A linchpin of DSST's model is a well-articulated set of standards. This creates a shared understanding about what the students should be learning and what the teachers should be teaching.

The staff at DSST invested significant time and resources into breaking down the standards into clear and measurable learning targets. They began by looking at the ACT College Readiness, the Common Core Standards, and most other widely accepted national content standards. They found that although these standards were a good place to start, the teachers had to figure out—to a very specific level—what they expected the students to learn and be able to do in order to graduate career- and college-ready. It wasn't easy to get each department and grade level to agree on exactly what the students should learn, but without this clarity, alignment of curriculum and assessments would have been impossible to achieve.

They also turned to the data to determine which of the standards were most frequently assessed on the ACT and state assessments. And when they did so, it became apparent that a lot less was assessed than they thought. This information led them to narrow down their standards to a set of DSST Power Standards. These would be the standards that absolutely every student had to master upon graduating from DSST. Figure 3.5 is the protocol they used to identify the Power Standards.

**Figure 3.5** Protocol for Identifying the Power Standards

Purpose: Teams identify which standards are most frequently assessed to create a set of Power Standards.

Step 1: Teams analyze test data to answer the following questions:

- Are there standards that are assessed and are not included in the current standards?
- Are there standards that are assessed at more than one grade level?
- Are there other significant changes that need to be made, based on what is being assessed?

Step 2: Teams determine which standards should be Power Standards by looking at the following criteria:

- Standards that appear on the assessment in at least two grade levels
- Standards that appear with the greatest frequency on the assessment
- Standards that should be taught in-depth in at least one grade level and then spiral progressively at higher levels

*(Continued)*

(Continued)

With a clear set of Power Standards, both the teachers and students are able to track their learning. They use daily mastery checks in which the students record what they have learned and what they still need to learn in order to meet the standard. There is never a question about the grades the students receive or where the students stand in relation to the standards—they keep track right along with the teacher.

## Coaching and Professional Development at DSST

Analyzing student assessment data is the center of coaching and professional development at DSST. Teachers regularly come together to tackle the questions, How are the students performing in relationship to the standards? and How can we make sure they all achieve these standards?

In addition to conversations about data, coaching and professional development addresses a specific set of instructional practices that the teachers are expected to use in their classrooms. These practices are brain based and engage adolescent learners. They include a decrease in a lecture-style delivery of content and an increase in written response and discussion, differentiation, and scaffolding instruction.

## An Embedded Coaching Model

Coaching is not invitational at DSST. It is seamlessly embedded into the school culture. The school has a tightly articulated set of expectations for both the students and teachers, and everyone knows what's expected. Coaching is a tool for making sure it happens.

Coaches at DSST are known as directors of curriculum and instruction. They work in direct partnership with the school director to support teachers through a process that includes

- goal setting based on data,
- informal observations,
- leading teachers through data analysis, and
- collaborative planning and instruction.

**Goal Setting Based on Data**—Goal setting is a formal process that involves the teacher, coach, and school director. They come together to set goals based on current assessment data, such as interim assessments and other formative measures. The data puts the students' needs front-and-center and creates the opportunity to design needs-based instruction that aligns with the school's core practices. The driving belief is that with support, each and every student can reach standards mastery.

**Informal Observations**–At DSST, teachers are not left alone until they are formally evaluated. Teachers are regularly observed and are provided with feedback. The intention is for the school to do whatever it takes to help teachers meet their goals for student learning. Issues around classroom culture, instructional planning, instructional practice, and assessment are the focus of the observations.

**Data Analysis Meetings**–Just following the interim or summative assessments, teachers meet in teams with the school director and coach to analyze the data. These conversations focus on measuring the success of the students by identifying red flags, discussing strategies for improving student performance, and identifying areas of future coaching support. Coaching is often an outcome of the data analysis meetings, because when the students' needs are identified, the natural next step is to design support to address whatever problems might exist. Chapter 5 includes an example of a data analysis meeting at DSST.

**Collaborative Planning and Instruction**–Another feature of coaching at DSST is supporting teachers in planning differentiated instruction. Coaching conversations are based on designing needs-based instruction, so providing differentiated instruction is a nonnegotiable. The students are heterogeneously grouped in their classes, and the teachers organize their instruction based on differentiated groupings or levels. An observer in any given classroom would see small groups of students working together on tasks that are designed to address their specific needs in relation to the standard.

## TAKING IT BEYOND A CHARTER SCHOOL IN DENVER

DSST is an example of an assess and deliver system. It has created a framework that is all about knowing where the students are, designing instruction that meets their needs, and then reassessing to make sure they are on target. It's a model that certainly isn't limited to a network of charter schools in Denver. All schools—whether charter, private, or public—can apply the following practices used by DSST:

- Establish clarity around each and every standard through the development of learning targets. With the adoption of the Common Core Standards, look closely to determine what it really means for students to reach mastery.
- Identify, or create, assessments that align with each standard. Determine a schedule for assessing students and arrange for teams to regularly analyze the data.
- Provide coaching support to teachers so they can design differentiated instruction that meets the needs of all students.

- Build in opportunities for students to self-evaluate and receive feedback about how they are doing in relationship to the standards.
- Establish a culture of achievement. Do not accept the premise that some students will achieve and others won't. Create the conditions for all students to graduate career- and college-ready.

## TOOLS AND TECHNIQUES

### Success Criteria Template

When I was a high school student, I didn't know what I was responsible for learning until the day of the test. It was a big guessing game. What should I study? What would I have to do to get an *A*? The success criteria that was introduced earlier in this chapter eliminates this uncertainty. Students know exactly what they need to learn and so does the teacher (Figure 3.6).

**Figure 3.6**   Success Criteria Template

| Standard: Student Outcomes | Date | Information I have heard of it. | Knowledge I can do this with help. | Know-How I can do this on my own. | Mastery I can teach someone else or apply the skill to a new situation. | Evidence of Learning I mastered this because I was able to teach ____. I did this on my own when I did ____. |
|---|---|---|---|---|---|---|
| | | | | | | |
| | | | | | | |
| | | | | | | |
| | | | | | | |
| | | | | | | |
| | | | | | | |
| | | | | | | |
| | | | | | | |

## IN SUMMARY

It can be difficult for coaches to find their place in a deliver and assess environment. There really isn't a role for coaches when teachers are wholly focused on covering content, testing students, and then moving on to new material.

Coaching becomes a necessity when we shift to an assess and deliver model of instruction. Teachers need support as they get clear on the standards by creating learning targets, designing formative assessments, analyzing the assessments, and planning differentiated instruction. For many, this is a new way of doing business in their classrooms that requires the support of a coach.

# 4 Measuring the Impact of Student-Centered Coaching

Educators from the boardroom to the classroom are interested in knowing how coaching, collaboration, and professional development positively impact students. We need to know this for several reasons. The first is obvious: without this information, we run the risk of making less-than-wise decisions about how to invest in education. Schools and districts may hire coaches with high hopes for increases in student achievement that never materialize. But it's not just about dollars and cents. It's also about efficacy. Coaches deserve to know that their work is making a difference where it counts—among the students.

## DESIGNING FOR IMPACT

A common belief among evaluators is that we can only indirectly measure the impact of coaching and collaboration on student learning. This should be no surprise, considering the fact that coaching has traditionally been designed to impact how teachers *teach* rather than how students *learn*. When coaching is solely focused on instructional practice, evaluating student learning feels like a stretch, leaving us with the same old tools for evaluating our work: teacher satisfaction surveys, observation checklists, and coaching logs that track how and where coaches are spending their time. While they may have some descriptive merit, these tools don't get at the question we all want answered: How has student learning changed as a result of coaching? If we want to go there, then we have to design our work differently. We have to design it with the students in mind.

Let's take a moment to revisit student-centered, teacher-centered, and relationship-driven coaching and the opportunities each present for measuring the impact of coaching on student and teacher learning (Figure 4.1).

**Figure 4.1** Measuring the Impact of Student-Centered, Teacher-Centered, and Relationship-Driven Coaching

More Impact on Students ———————————————— Less Impact on Students

| | Student-Centered Coaching | Teacher-Centered Coaching | Relationship-Driven Coaching |
|---|---|---|---|
| **Purpose** | Increase student learning through the use of effective teaching practices. | Implement effective teaching practices. | Provide needs-based support to teachers. |
| **What Is Measured?** | Student learning and teaching practice are measured in relation to one another. By impacting student learning, we can impact teaching practice as well. | Teaching practice is measured based on the fidelity of implementation. The theory is that improvement in teaching will lead to improvement in student learning. | Teachers' attitudes about the coaching are measured. |
| **Measurement Tools** | • Results-Based Coaching Tool (Figure 4.3) <br> • Assessment checklists based on learning targets <br> • Common Core Standards <br> • Coaching logs <br> • Observation checklists <br> • Teacher participation logs | • Coaching logs <br> • Observation checklists <br> • Teacher satisfaction surveys <br> • Teacher participation logs | • Teacher satisfaction surveys <br> • Teacher participation logs |

## USING THE RESULTS-BASED COACHING TOOL TO MEASURE STUDENT AND TEACHER LEARNING

The school board for the St. Joseph School District in Missouri wanted proof that coaching was making a difference for their students—a fair

, given the fact that the district had invested significant resources
re eighteen instructional coaches across their elementary, middle, and
.igh schools. At the time, I was working with the team in St. Joseph, and
it was up to me to create a tool to capture the impact that the coaches were
making. I decided not to settle for the argument that we can't link coaching with student achievement and went about creating a system that
would help the coaches in St. Joseph capture the data they needed.

I knew I had to be sensitive to the fact that the coaches in St. Joseph had
their hands full. I didn't want to add to their workload and knew that
whatever I came up with had to reinforce their coaching practice and fit
seamlessly into their daily work. I also wanted to be sure that something
empirical came from the data so that we could present the school board
with the hard data they were requesting.

Many of the pieces were already in place. The coaches had been carefully
selected based on their knowledge and skills. I had worked with them on an
ongoing basis to get their coaching up and running, and many were implementing coaching cycles in their schools. They were dedicated coaches and
spent a good amount of time with teachers. Whatever evaluation system we
chose had to tap into what existed, so I bookended the basic structure of the
coaching cycle with pre- and post-assessments to come up with the following framework for documenting the coaches' impact (Figure 4.2).

**Figure 4.2**  Capturing Data Across a Coaching Cycle

| At the Beginning of the Coaching Cycle | | During the Coaching Cycle | | At the End of the Coaching Cycle | |
|---|---|---|---|---|---|
| Coach and Teacher: | Coach and Teacher: | Coach and Teacher: | Coach and Teacher: | Coach: | Coach and Teacher: |
| Identify an overarching goal for student learning along with a clear set of learning targets: "Students will learn . . ." | Pre-assess students to determine how they are doing in relation to the learning targets. | Design a set of instructional practices that specifically link to the learning targets. | Work together to implement the instructional practices and reflect on how those practices are moving students toward the learning targets. | Observe the teacher to identify the instructional practices that are being implemented. | Post-assess students to measure their performance in relation to the learning targets. |

When I presented this model to the coaches, they reacted just as I'd hoped. They were thrilled to have a nonthreatening tool to measure their impact. They felt that it reinforced the types of conversations they were having with teachers and provided a natural flow and rhythm that they could repeat again and again. Rather than becoming a distraction to their work, they recognized how it would help scaffold their development as coaches. They could see themselves having these conversations with teachers and confessed that they had been feeling their way through most of their coaching conversations and weren't sure how their work was affecting the students.

Our next step was to make the evaluation process more concrete and help the coaches implement it as a natural addition to their coaching cycles. While they liked the framework, they also wanted an organized place to capture their work. We created the Results-Based Coaching Tool to do just that (Figure 4.3).

## FIRST THINGS FIRST: IDENTIFYING A GOAL FOR STUDENT LEARNING

The first step in using the Results-Based Coaching Tool is to identify a goal for student learning. Framing coaching around a student-centered goal shifts coaching away from fixing the teacher and toward creating a partnership that is about working together to ensure that the students reach standards mastery. The teacher may choose to target a whole class, a section of students, or a subgroup that is in need of extra attention. More often than not, the goal is derived directly from standards such as the Common Core Standards. Other times, it may relate more to student engagement or classroom culture. Figure 4.4 provides examples of goals for student learning.

When teachers are new to student-centered coaching, they often think it will focus directly on what they do. It can take a bit of practice for coaches to learn how to gracefully shift the focus away from the teacher and toward a goal for the students. The example in Figure 4.5 provides a glimpse into how a skilled coach maneuvers through a goal-setting conversation with a high school science teacher.

## COLLECTING BASELINE DATA

Once Stacy and Todd had established a goal for student learning, they were ready to determine where the students were in relation to the

| | Coach's Name: | | | |
|---|---|---|---|---|
| **Coaching Cycle Focus:**<br>Circle One: Small Group or One-on-One Cycle | **Dates:**<br>_____ to _____<br>_____<br>beginning date ending date | | | |
| *What are the learning targets?*<br>*How will the students be pre-assessed?* | *What instructional practices will produce the desired outcomes?* | *What coaching practices were implemented during the coaching cycle?*<br>*(check all that apply)* | *As a result of the coaching cycle, what instructional practices are being used on a consistent basis?* | *To what degree did the students meet the learning targets?* |
| 1. **Learning Targets and Pre-Assessment** | 2. **Instructional Practices** | 3. **Coaching Practices** | 4. **Changes to the Teaching Practice** | 5. **Changes to Student Learning** |
| *Students will ...*<br>**Baseline Data:**<br>___% of students were proficient.<br>___% of students were partially proficient.<br>___% of students were not proficient.<br>Number of students<br>_____ | | ☐ Analysis of student work<br>☐ Collaborative planning<br>☐ Co-teaching<br>☐ Observation of the teacher with feedback<br>☐ Demonstration Teaching<br>☐ Professional Learning Communities (PLC)<br>☐ Team planning<br>☐ Observation in other classrooms<br>☐ Professional study, reading, and discussion | | **Post-Assessment Data:**<br>___% of students are proficient.<br>___% of students are partially proficient.<br>___% of students are not proficient.<br>Overall growth:<br>_____ % |

**Figure 4.4** Goals for Student Learning

| Standards-Based Goals | • Students will interpret parts of an expression, such as terms, factors, and coefficients (Common Core Standard A-SSE.1).<br>• Students will compare and contrast the information gained from experiments, simulations, videos, or multimedia sources with that gained from reading a text on the same topic (Common Core Standard RST.6–8.9).<br>• Students will determine two or more themes or central ideas of a text and analyze their development over the course of the text, including how they interact and build on one another to produce a complex account; students will provide an objective summary of the text (Common Core Standard RL.11–12.2). |
|---|---|
| Student Engagement Goals | • Students will regularly contribute when working in small groups.<br>• Students will use strategies for productive dialogue when discussing new learning.<br>• Students will stop and synthesize several times during a course period. |
| Student Behavior Goals | • Students will complete the assigned task.<br>• Students will ask questions when they do not understand the assigned task.<br>• Students will self-evaluate their progress relative to the learning target. |

**Figure 4.5** Identifying a Goal for Student Learning

| | |
|---|---|
| **Todd (coach):** | Thanks for meeting with me today. This is our first chance to talk about our coaching cycle. Can you tell me what you'd like to focus on in our work together? |
| **Stacy (teacher):** | Sure. I want to do a better job formatively assessing my students. I know that we are supposed to be doing this, and I'm not sure how to get started. |
| **Todd:** | Great. Can you give me a bit of background on how you arrived at this goal and where you want to go with it? |
| **Stacy:** | I've been learning about how to use formative assessments such as exit slips and short writing tasks in science. I'd like to figure out how to use these ideas in my classes so I have less to grade but still know where my kids are. |

*(Continued)*

**Figure 4.5** (Continued)

| | |
|---|---|
| **Todd:** | You are so right that it is about knowing where your kids are. That really is the basis for formative assessment. Can we take a minute to think about where you want them to be at this point in the year? What are your goals for your students in terms of the biology content you are teaching? |
| **Stacy:** | Well, okay. I am working with my biology class on cellular reproduction. The expectation is for the students to learn the differences between the stages of mitosis and meiosis. To do that, we will have to get into cell cycle, DNA, genes, and chromosomes. . . . |
| **Todd:** | It sounds like you have a pretty clear vision for where you want to go with the unit. What if we tackled your science content and still addressed the questions you have about formative assessment? We can frame our work around your science unit so we stay student centered. What if we set a goal like this: "Students will understand the differences between the stages of mitosis and meiosis"? |
| **Stacy:** | I guess I'm okay with that. But there is a ton of vocabulary I have to teach as well. I need to be sure that I get to everything. And I need some ideas about activities we can do. |
| **Todd:** | Absolutely; we will have lots of opportunities to decide what specifically you will teach, including the vocabulary. As you know, learning targets are a big part of the curriculum planning that we do at our school. We can take that goal and create some learning targets to match it. We can also do a formative pre-assessment to see what your students already know. |
| **Stacy:** | Okay. Can we meet again this Friday to plan some lessons? I really want to get going with this on Monday. |
| **Todd:** | Yes; as soon as we have the pre-assessment, the lesson planning will fall into place. |
| **Stacy:** | Sounds good to me. Thanks. |

*Baseline data*

goal. Stacy hoped that some of her students would have some background in the subject matter, because it had been introduced in previous years. Todd said, "Great; let's capture what they already know. That will become our baseline data so we can track their growth over the next four weeks."

Stacy suggested a short quiz . . . and in the next breath, she worried that some of her students would stress out if they had to take a quiz on material they hadn't learned yet. Todd suggested that they call it a *knowledge check* instead of a quiz. Stacy could make it clear to the students that they wouldn't be graded on the assignment but that it would help her decide what to focus on in the unit. Stacy felt good about this approach, especially since it aligned with her goal to use more types of formative assessment in her classroom. They dug in to the district curriculum and standards to create the following pre-assessment (Figure 4.6).

**Figure 4.6**   Pre-Assessment for Mitosis and Meiosis

1. Explain the differences between mitosis and meiosis, including the stages.
2. Draw a picture that represents mitosis.
3. Draw a picture that represents meiosis.
4. Explain how a child would be affected if the parent's cells did not undergo meiosis?
5. List as many vocabulary words as you can that are relevant to mitosis and meiosis.

After they identified the questions, Stacy asked, "This is great, but what should I do with them? I mean, how will I score their papers, since I don't plan to use them for a grade?"

Todd said, "That's our next step. Let's think about it in terms of what it would look like if the students demonstrated that they were proficient in their knowledge of the differences between mitosis and meiosis." They took about ten more minutes to develop the following criteria (Figure 4.7).

**Figure 4.7**   Learning Targets for the Pre-Assessment on Mitosis and Meiosis

- The students demonstrate that they understand that mitosis and meiosis are two different things.
- The students are able to compare and contrast the stages of mitosis and meiosis.
- The students understand that mitosis and meiosis relate to cellular reproduction.
- The students understand the impact that mitosis and meiosis have on the human body.
- The students are able to draw representations of mitosis and meiosis.
- The students understand at least five vocabulary words that are used in reference to mitosis and meiosis.

It was Friday afternoon, and Todd and Stacy were running out of steam. Todd asked if she felt good about what she'd do on Monday. Stacy nodded and said that she'd give the pre-assessment—or *knowledge check*—on Monday. Then they could meet again on Tuesday to look at what the students did and plan some instruction.

## PLANNING BASED ON STUDENT WORK

For many teachers, planning is about deciding what content to cover, in what order, and using what types of activities. In a student-centered model, planning almost always involves the analysis of student evidence, such as writing samples, problems, written reflections, or anecdotal evidence from observing and talking with students. We simply have to know where the students are in relation to where they need to be before we can make any decisions about what to teach. These conversations take place on a weekly basis either with an individual teacher or a team of teachers.

When Todd and Stacy came back together, they began by looking at how the students did on the pre-assessment. Stacy laid a stack of student papers on the table, and Todd pulled out the learning targets. Together, they sorted the student work into three piles: (1) students who were proficient, (2) students who were partially proficient, and (3) students who demonstrated little-to-no knowledge about mitosis and meiosis.

They were surprised by what they found. There were three students in the proficient group. Stacy was thrilled, given the fact that she hasn't even taught the unit yet. The partially proficient group included most of her class (18 students). The last group, with little-to-no knowledge about the subject, included seven students.

It didn't take long for Stacy to kick into planning mode. She said, "Okay, so I obviously have to figure out how to meet these different needs. I can't expect the three proficient students to do the same work as the others." Todd agreed and wondered aloud if they might be able to create some different assignments for those students. The proficient students could engage in some work using the microscopes and Internet. Perhaps Stacy could design a real-world problem to be solved, so they could apply what they knew and learn more. They decided to call this group *Level 3*.

The middle group would receive instruction based on their prevailing needs. Stacy and Todd took a closer look at the pre-assessment and decided that they would begin by teaching the students how to draw the phases of mitosis and meiosis. In this way, they would target the expectation that the students understand the stages, how they compared, and the key vocabulary words. They decided to call this group *Level 2*.

Some of the students in the last group were Second Language Learners and Stacy wanted to make sure that whatever they did was supported with visuals and lots of opportunities for conversation. They decided that this group would do the same work as the Level 2 group but would be supplemented with videos and more intensive support regarding the key vocabulary words.

Stacy had always been a teacher who worked hard to meet the needs of her students. Her struggle had been knowing what those needs were. By analyzing and sorting the student work, Stacy now had a vision for how to design student-centered instruction that would move everyone forward.

## CAPTURING TEACHER GROWTH    *change in instructional practices*

Evaluating the impact of coaching also rests in documenting a set of practices that we hope to see the teachers use as a result of their collaboration with the coach. Some coaches think about this in terms of whether a teacher is using a set of instructional practices with fidelity, and others turn to a checklist of best practices to gauge their work. The idea is that, with coaching support, teachers will become more skillful in their use of effective instructional pedagogy, or, as Jan Miller Burkins (2007) puts it, "The instruction in our school is the most honest feedback on our work we will ever receive" (p. 152).

There is no question that it is of the utmost importance for a teacher and coach to understand the changes to instruction that have occurred as a result of their work together. They have invested time and energy into their collaboration, and it would be sensible to expect that some new practices would be firmly established during that time. What makes me uneasy is the thought of dictating to teachers which specific practices I think they should be using with their students, especially in content areas that I've never taught. Instead, I prefer to tap into the teachers' goals for their students in order to open the doors to conversations about practices that might move their learning forward. Once these have been established, we can document if and how they are used.

### Using Instructional Checklists

Instructional checklists are everywhere. They may be a district's scope and sequence, a framework for teacher evaluation, a rubric for instruction, or a list of core practices.

I have learned to be careful about how I use these tools. If I view my role as making teachers do all of the things that are on the checklist, then I may damage our relationship. After all, as their coach, I am not there to hold them accountable for doing these things. That is the job of the principal. Instead, I like to use instructional checklists as a resource, a collection of ideas that we can draw from to meet our goals for student learning.

## CAPTURING STUDENT GROWTH

If we want to know how students grow as a result of our coaching work, we can't stop at the instructional practices that the teacher is using. We have to capture student growth as well. I take a pragmatic approach to this part of the process. To measure student growth, I often pull out the pre-assessment to use again at the end of the coaching cycle to measure student growth.

After a few weeks of analyzing student work and collaboratively planning instruction, Stacy and Todd wanted to know what the students had learned. They wanted to know how close the students were to reaching the learning targets so they could determine if the students were ready to move on. They gave the same assessment, but this time it would count for a grade.

As they analyzed the final assessment, Stacy hoped that the proficient pile would be quite a bit larger than it was at the beginning of the coaching cycle. Todd hoped the same thing. Originally, there were three students in the proficient category; this is to be expected, given the fact that this was new content to most of the students. Now, there were 18 students in the proficient category—an increase of 54%. The partially proficient group included seven students—most of whom had correct responses on some, but not all, of the questions on the assessment. The group of students who were not able to demonstrate a clear understanding of the content included three students. Stacy noted that one of these students had a terrible attendance rate, another student struggled with English, and the last one was someone Stacy had been working with in an after-school tutoring program.

Stacy and Todd knew that they weren't done, and talked at length about how they would provide additional support to the students who weren't quite there yet. But for now, they felt pretty good. Finals were in three weeks, and the vast majority of the students had demonstrated mastery of the learning targets.

Todd turned to Stacy and asked, "So, how do you feel about the growth?"

Stacy smiled with an easy answer, "It's fantastic. Working with you changed how I teach. Now, I understand how easy it is to embed formative assessment into my daily practice. I learned how to teach in a way that directly meets my students' needs, and it paid off." She continued, "Can we do it again with my genetics unit? This time I'd like the rest of my team to participate. I thought that since we have the same time for prep, we might was well include them."

Todd was glad that Stacy saw the value in working with a coach, but even more important was how good she felt about the students' progress. To Todd, this was the best feedback he could hope for. Now he would have to figure out how to do it again, this time with her whole team.

## MEASURING THE IMPACT OF SMALL-GROUP COLLABORATION

Measuring growth across an individual coaching cycle is similar to documenting the work that occurs with small groups. The primary difference comes down to identifying a shared goal for student learning. It is quite easy for teams to agree upon a goal when they teach the same course to the same grade level. However, this isn't always the case. For example, Stacy's team included teachers from the same grade level who taught different courses. Todd had to figure out a way to move them through the process in a way aligned with their specific standards. It would be a bit more challenging than working with a single teacher, but the potential for impact is far greater and well worth it.

**Teams With a Shared Instructional Focus**—Teachers look to the student data, standards, and curriculum to identify a shared goal for student learning. They meet with the coach as a team to create learning targets, analyze student work, plan instruction, and create ways to formatively assess students. The coach rotates between the teachers' classrooms to provide instructional support and monitor how students are progressing. To document the impact on the teachers and students, the coach maintains a separate Results-Based Coaching Tool for each teacher in the group. Three to four teachers is the ideal number for this type of coaching cycle.

**Teams From Different Grade Levels or Instructional Foci**—Teachers work with the coach to set individual goals for their students, based on their own standards and grade-level expectations. They meet with the coach as a team to analyze work from their own classes and use their own learning targets. The coach rotates between the teachers' classrooms to provide instructional support and monitor how students are progressing. To document the impact on the teachers and students, the coach maintains a separate Results-Based Coaching Tool for each teacher in the group. Two to three teachers is the ideal number for this type of coaching cycle.

## TOOLS AND TECHNIQUES

By using the Results-Based Coaching Tool, Todd was able to document the impact of coaching on the teaching and learning that was taking place in Stacy's classroom. Figure 4.8 shows all that was accomplished in a few short weeks.

Stacy and Todd's Results-Based Coaching Tool

| Teacher Name(s): Stacy | | Coach's Name: Todd | | |
|---|---|---|---|---|
| **Coaching Cycle Focus:** <br> Circle One: Small Group (or One-on-One) Cycle | | **Dates:** <br> *October 10* to *October 31* <br> **beginning date    ending date** | | |
| *What are the learning targets? How will the students be pre-assessed?* | *What instructional practices will produce the desired outcomes?* | *What coaching practices were implemented during the coaching cycle?* <br> *(check all that apply)* | *As a result of the coaching cycle, what instructional practices are being used on a consistent basis?* | *To what degree did the students meet the learning targets?* |
| 1. **Learning Targets and Pre-Assessment** | 2. **Instructional Practices** | 3. **Coaching Practices** | 4. **Changes to the Teaching Practice** | 5. **Changes to Student Learning** |
| Students will understand the differences between mitosis and meiosis. <br><br> Baseline Data: <br><br> 10% (3/28) were proficient. <br><br> 64% (18/28) were partially proficient. <br><br> 25% (7/28) were not proficient. | Differentiating instruction using a system of levels (1, 2, 3) <br><br> Visuals: video, simulations, and models <br><br> Vocabulary that is directly tied to visuals, simulations, and models <br><br> Exit slips and other ways to formatively assess students | *Coaching practices that were used:* <br> ✓ Analysis of student work <br> ✓ Collaborative planning <br> ✓ Co-teaching <br> ✓ Observation of the teacher with feedback <br><br> *Coaching practices that were not used:* <br> -Demonstration Teaching <br> -Professional Learning Communities (PLC) <br> -Team planning <br> -Observation in other classrooms <br> -Professional study, reading, and discussion | Differentiating instruction using a system of levels (1, 2, 3). Note: Stacy is still refining these practices. <br><br> Visuals: video, simulations, and models <br><br> Vocabulary that is directly tied to visuals, simulations, and models <br><br> Exit slips and other ways to formatively assess students | Post-Assessment Data: <br><br> 64% (18/28) were proficient. <br><br> 25% (7/28) were partially proficient. <br><br> 10% (3/28) were not proficient. <br><br> Overall Growth: <br><br> 54% increase in the proficient group. |

### Designing Assessments for the Results-Based Coaching Tool

Designing the pre- and post-assessment can take some creativity on the part of the teacher and coach. The following ideas for assessments include standards-based goals for student learning, goals focused on student engagement, and goals related to student behavior (Figure 4.9).

**Figure 4.9** Sample Assessments

|  | Goal | Pre- and Post-Assessments |
|---|---|---|
| **Standards-Based Goal for Student Learning** | Students will interpret parts of an expression, such as terms, factors, and coefficients (Common Core Standard A-SSE.1). | Students solve a series of problems that focus on the areas to be assessed. |
|  | Students will determine two or more themes or central ideas of a text and analyze their development over the course of the text, including how they interact and build on one another to produce a complex account; students will provide an objective summary of the text (Common Core Standard RL.11–12.2). | Students read a short text and write a written summary that provides a complex account of what they read. |
|  | Students will compare and contrast the information gained from experiments, simulations, videos, or multimedia sources with that gained from reading a text on the same topic (Common Core Standard RST.6–8.9). | Students write a reflection to compare and contrast two sources (i.e., text and video or text and experiment). |
| **Goal Focusing on Student Engagement** | Students will regularly contribute when working in small groups. | Students work together in groups while the teacher and coach observe. |
|  | Students will use strategies for productive dialogue when discussing new learning. | During instructional time, the teacher and coach observe how students engage in dialogue with one another. |
|  | Students will stop and synthesize several times during a course period. | While learning new content, students use a note-taking tool to synthesize their learning. |
| **Goal Focusing on Student Behavior** | Students will complete the assigned task. | Teacher and coach track task completion. |
|  | Students will ask questions when they do not understand the assigned task. | Teacher and coach track the regularity and quality of student questions. |
|  | Students will self-evaluate their progress relative to the learning target. | Students write a reflection of where they are as a learner. |

## IN SUMMARY

When you are a coach, it is hard to settle for measuring coaching based only on teaching practice. It just doesn't feel like enough. While I wholeheartedly agree that there are a collection of effective teaching practices that we would like to see teachers using, I'm not comfortable making the assumption that if these practices are in place, then the students are learning.

This chapter introduced a framework to design coaching in a way that provides opportunities to document both teacher and student learning across a coaching cycle. If we don't design our work with an eye toward capturing impact, we simply won't know what we've accomplished.

Previously, Stacy used a set of activities to conceptualize the concept of mitosis and meiosis. Her interest in formative assessments indicated that she wanted to provide her students with more targeted instruction. When she and Todd analyzed the pre-assessments, her thinking was confirmed. She knew she had to think differently about her instruction, and Todd helped her do that with an eye on the content she was expected to teach. Student-centered coaching led to student-centered instruction, and they were able to document it all.

# 5 Leading the Coaching Effort

I'd like to begin this chapter by acknowledging that principals are busy people, especially secondary principals. Delegation isn't simply a matter of good management; it's a matter of survival. And when a principal is lucky enough to have a coach, it often provides an enormous sense of relief to think that someone is tending to all of the work that needs to be done around teaching and learning so that the principal can deal with discipline, data, testing, parents, and all of the activities that secondary schools offer.

Here's the thing: delegating a coaching effort doesn't work. A coach can't singlehandedly take care of the work to be done around teaching and learning, because a coach is not the school leader. Their roles are different. School leaders supervise and evaluate teachers, while a coach is a peer to teachers. School leaders set the vision, and the coach provides support to make it happen. When it comes to a coaching effort, leadership is required.

Let's pause for a moment to consider the word *leadership*. You may think about school leadership as an individual person, such as a principal. Or if you work in a larger school, you may view leadership as a team consisting of the principal, assistant principals, and deans. In this chapter, I will use the terms *school leader*, *leadership*, and *principal* interchangeably. How you define who this involves is up to you and will probably be based on the organization, size, and resources of your school.

## MERGING ACCOUNTABILITY AND SUPPORT

One of the most persistent roadblocks in establishing a successful coaching effort is confusion around expectations and accountability. I rarely encounter a school where everyone knows what is expected and how they will be held accountable.

Ambiguity around expectations for teaching and learning is lethal for coaching. When teachers have different ideas about what the students should be learning and the teaching practices they should be using, they often operate as if they are independent contractors, and the school loses its sense of cohesion and focus. I refer to this as the *hairdresser effect*, because sometimes, teachers believe that they should be treated as if they are renting space in a school rather than operating as an organization that is working toward a singular vision.

When the expectations around teaching and learning aren't clear, coaches are unsure about how hard they should be pushing teachers to improve, especially those teachers who aren't meeting the needs of their students. Should the coach report the issues to the principal and hope they are addressed? Should the coach put pressure on the teachers to recognize that a problem exists? Or should the coach avoid the teachers who aren't responding and focus on teachers with whom he or she has established trust?

Establishing clarity around how coaching and accountability work together is vital to a coaching effort because clarity creates conditions in which coaches understand their role and, in turn, are in a position to directly benefit the students. The following examples illustrate differing levels of accountability and support and how they impact a coaching effort.

## Schools With High Levels of Accountability and Support

In schools with high levels of accountability and support, teachers know what is expected. They aren't left to their own devices, but instead, they understand that they are a part of a larger system that is oriented around the needs of the students. A well-articulated partnership exists between the principal and coach, and they have a shared understanding of what's taking place in classrooms so that they have the information they need to develop a plan that meets teachers where they are, and moves them forward.

The use of data is intrinsic to a high-accountability and high-support system. When student learning is closely monitored, it becomes easier to identify where the students are in relation to the standards. When data isn't a part of the conversation, we lose sight of where the students are in relation to where they need to be.

Establishing a model with high accountability and support requires skill on the part of both the school leader and coach. It would be a mistake to assume that principals step into the job knowing how to effectively use a coach. It would also be a mistake to assume that coaches understand how to design their work to be student centered and results based. Rather, the principal and coach work side-by-side to create a shared understanding of how coaching fits with their vision for how the school can improve.

Sometimes we mistake high accountability with a model based on fear or compliance. The teachers' decision making may be diminished through the use of "teacher-proof" materials or pacing guides. The assumption is that if we take control away from the teachers, we can better manage what they do each day in their classrooms. This approach leaves coaches with very little opportunity to provide high levels of support, because teacher decision making has been eliminated. A model based on fear and compliance is a high-accountability and low-support model, since there is little room for coaching or instructional decision making. The most obvious downside to this approach is that teachers have less ability to meet the individual needs of their students, because they are expected to blindly follow along with a predetermined curriculum or set of materials.

## Schools With Moderate Levels of Accountability and Support

In schools with moderate levels of accountability and support, it may be unclear who is responsible for holding teachers accountable. This in turn puts coaches in the position of being unsure about their role.

Christina, a middle school coach I have worked with over the past few years, is in a school with moderate levels of accountability and support. Even though she has been a coach for several years, she is still somewhat unclear about what is expected of the teachers. Other than the accountability that is provided by test scores and the use of certain materials, the expectations are hard to pin down.

She gets along well with her principal and meets with him on a weekly basis. During these conversations, they discuss schoolwide professional development, coaching, and professional learning community (PLC) sessions. Her principal often turns to her for information about how teachers are doing, because he is so tied up with meetings and other obligations that he spends little time in classrooms. On the surface, it seems that everyone in the school is happy, and many of the students are performing pretty well. But Christina worries about a certain population of students who are underperforming. She has tried to put her finger on the causes for this lack of student performance, but she feels that it is really something that her principal should be spearheading. She has tried to share her concerns that there are pockets of teachers who aren't on board and pockets of students who aren't doing well, but she can't seem to get anywhere during these discussions.

Christina's school is not unique. In fact, I run into schools with moderate levels of accountability and support all the time. They are everywhere.

As Christina is finding, the lack of accountability in her school limits the impact she can make on both the students and teachers.

### Schools With Low Levels of Accountability and Support

A particularly challenging place for coaching to take root is in schools with low levels of accountability. In these cases, there is no partnership between the coach and school leader and teachers simply choose not to participate. Coaching becomes more about providing resources and non-threatening support to teachers, and it tends to impact pockets of teachers rather than the full faculty.

Imagine a well-intentioned and highly trained coach who is placed in this situation. The coach most likely knows where the instruction isn't meeting the needs of students but has no leverage to do anything about it. The downside is fairly obvious: coaches never last long and nothing improves for the students. Low accountability and low support simply won't get you anywhere. Coaches in these schools are caught between a rock and a hard place because they understand that they don't have the support they need to make an impact.

## WHAT'S OUR FOCUS?

Each of the examples within this book share one thing in common—a clearly identified focus for student learning. With a clear focus, the coach can engage teachers in something that they perceive is expected and meaningful. In smaller schools, the focus may be shared across a full faculty; in larger, more comprehensive schools, the focus may be specific to departments or grade levels. In either case, the focus is authentic to teachers, so they can see a clear connection to how it will impact their students.

Coming up with a focus isn't the hard part. Schools today are so rich in data that it takes very little time looking at how students are performing in order to identify a focus for student learning. The challenge is maintaining the focus over time and holding teachers accountable. As you continue to read this chapter, you will be introduced to a variety of leadership practices that are designed to do just that.

## DRIVEN BY DATA ANALYSIS

Stefan is the director of the middle school on the Stapleton campus of Denver School of Science and Technology (DSST). Originally a science

teacher at the school, Stefan is now knee-deep in data and instr
decision making. Brianna, also a former teacher at the school, is tʃ
tor of curriculum and instruction and provides coaching, leadership, and
data-driven support to teachers.

It was early December, and Stefan and Brianna had hardly had a
chance to catch their breath as they rotated through a series of data
analysis meetings with teams of teachers. As Stefan got started with a team
from the math department, he reminded the teachers that their objective was to analyze data from the recent interim assessment and the
midyear growth measure, the Measures of Academic Progress (MAP),
in order to flag instructional and student concerns. Stefan used the following questions to guide the teams through the analysis of the data
(Figure 5.1).

**Figure 5.1** Guiding Questions for Data Analysis Meetings

1. What does the data reveal?

   Highlight the 3–5 most significant data points or trends—red flags—that you see
   in this set of results.

2. What questions does the data pose?

   For each red flag that you've identified, generate 2–3 questions that the data
   raises for you.

3. What might explain the data?

   For each red flag, jot down any theories you have about causes/explanations for
   the data.

4. What will we do about it?

   For each red flag, identify instructional strategies to improve student
   achievement.

As they met with the team from the math department, Stefan and
Brianna noticed that a large group of students had underperformed on
the midyear interim assessment. Rather than overlooking these grades
and moving on to the next unit, Stefan wanted to know why this happened and what they were going to do about it. He began the conversation with the following questions:

- Does what you are teaching align with the assessment?
- Was the instruction differentiated to meet the needs of students
  with differing knowledge or background?
- Did the teachers spiral back to catch students with misconceptions
  or gaps in their learning?

It turned out that due to some recent revisions on the interim assessment, the teachers had been focusing on a wholly different set of learning targets than on what was being assessed. With this lack of alignment between the curriculum and assessment, it was no surprise that so many students had underperformed.

Stefan immediately recognized that he had better get the teachers some coaching to redesign their curriculum. Since Brianna's background was in the humanities, he recruited Kathy, a teacher and math department chair, to help out. She worked with the teachers to rewrite the curriculum they had been teaching, create a plan for differentiating their lessons, and design some new formative assessments. She also helped them plan how they would spiral back to the learning targets that the students may have missed the first time around.

This conversation simply wouldn't have been possible without the data. The data provided Stefan with the leverage he needed to hold the teachers accountable to address concerns around student learning. While DSST has a fairly refined data system, some districts have data systems that aren't so seamless. Sometimes a data system is flawed because it is trying to measure too much, is assessing material that hasn't been taught, doesn't align with the standards, or teachers don't understand the purpose for the assessments and feel that they will be blamed for student failure. This presents an obvious challenge to school leaders. Should they disavow the data? Try to work with what they have? Or should they defer the question of measuring student growth to teachers?

Some schools and districts have turned to DuFour, Eaker, and DuFour's (2005) model of PLCs to create their own assessments and monitor student growth. This approach occurs within teams and is described in the following way:

> When teacher teams develop common formative assessments throughout the school year, each teacher can identify how his or her students performed on each skill compared with other students. Individual teachers can call on their team colleagues to help them reflect on areas of concern. Each teacher has access to the ideas, materials, strategies, and talents of the entire team. (p. 40)

Whatever system we create, we need interim assessments that are formal and standards based. We also need formative, or on-the-spot, assessments that measure a clear set of learning targets. When this is the case, we are in the position to identify progress (or a lack of it) so that the teachers are able to respond immediately to the needs of their students.

# LEADERS KNOW GOOD INSTRUCTION WHEN THEY SEE IT

If we subscribe to the belief that the school leaders' primary responsibility is to promote teaching and learning, then school leaders had better be able to recognize high-quality teaching and learning when they see it. Imagine other professions, such as operating a restaurant, leading a soccer team, or running a law firm. We can make the assumption that if these endeavors were indeed successful, then the leader knew a thing or two about the skills involved in making it happen. The person operating the restaurant knows how to cook. The coach knows how to play soccer. The attorney knows how to practice law. The same is true for school leaders. The school leader must know what high-quality instruction looks like in order to make sure it is in place throughout the school.

It wouldn't be sensible to imply that a school leader in a large secondary school should know the content knowledge for every course. I'd challenge you to come across someone who knows the content for economics, French, world history, R.O.T.C., art, and so on. That's never going to happen. Instead, let's consider the role of the school leader as understanding the pedagogy (or the use of instructive strategies) rather than the knowledge of the content itself. In this case, the school leader is prepared to recognize high-quality instruction when it exists and know what to do if it doesn't.

Recognizing high-quality instruction also means that the school leader, or a member of the leadership team, is in classrooms on a regular basis. The dilemma is how to pull this off without killing themselves, especially in large secondary schools.

Kim Marshall tackles this challenge in his book, *Rethinking Teacher Supervision and Evaluation* (2009). He advocates for designing a system of unannounced mini-observations in which an administrator spends approximately ten minutes observing instruction. You may wonder why only ten minutes, when most observations by school leaders last far longer. Marshall argues that there is an "inverse relationship between the length of each visit and the number of classrooms administrators will be able to visit on a regular basis" (p. 68). His target is to observe teachers approximately 12–19 times across a school year by completing 3 to 5 mini-observations each day. He could never accomplish this with longer observations.

While in the classroom, Marshall moves around the room, listens to students, examines their work, and considers what to discuss with the teacher later on. He asks himself, "What strikes me in here? What's interesting, different, or problematic? What is worth sharing with the teacher? What will give this teacher a new insight?" (p. 50).

Feedback is a necessary component of Marshall's model. Without feedback, the teacher is left wondering what the principal thought and doesn't receive the information that is necessary to get better. Marshall doesn't suggest that principals sit at their desks and write up elaborate feedback for teachers. Instead, he has found that making the time for a short face-to-face conversation provides him with the opportunity to share some words of praise, reinforcement, and suggestions without the homework. By observing teachers many times across the year, he finds that he can gain a more detailed view of what's going on in the classrooms, which in turn impacts his ability to lead.

## CLARIFYING ROLES

It isn't uncommon for a principal and coach to have very different ideas about coaching. Therefore, it is often necessary for the coach and school leader to have a conversation to clarify their roles. The principal and coach can craft a partnership right from the start by discussing the following points:

1. What is the focus for improvement? Identifying a focus for improvement provides direction for the school leader, the coach, and the teachers. Key questions include What does the data say our students should be doing better? and Where would teachers benefit from support regarding instructional practice?

2. How will we collaborate? What lies in the domain of the leadership, what lies in the domain of the coach, and where is there overlap? I use a Venn diagram to get specific about how the leadership and coach will work together.

3. When will we collaborate? When will we sit down together to plan and problem solve? I suggest a weekly meeting between the administration and coach. An example of a meeting between a principal and coach is provided later in this chapter.

Figure 5.2 provides a tool for documenting an initial conversation between the school leader and coach. It leads the principal and coach through a discussion of important decisions about the focus of professional development, their respective roles in enacting the professional development, and agreements about principal and coach communication.

**Figure 5.2** Principal/Coach Agreement

Principal:

Coach:

Date:

I. Establishing a Focus

   – Use student data to identify an area where students are underperforming. Set this as the priority for teacher and student learning.

   – Establish how data will be used to monitor growth.

II. Defining Roles

   – Use the Venn diagram to determine how the role of the coach will look in relationship to the role of the principal.

   – Determine how the coaching role will be introduced and reinforced.

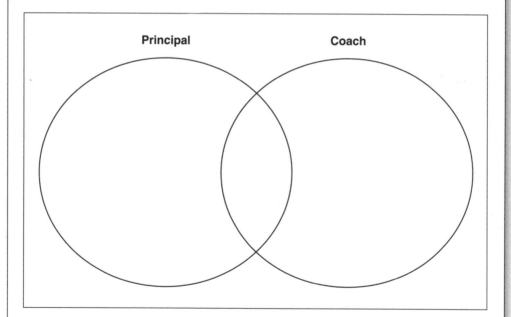

III. Setting Up Ongoing Communication and Scheduling

   – Determine how and when the principal and coach will communicate.

   – Determine what the coach's schedule will look like.

   – Determine how the principal and coach will support each other.

## A CASE IN POINT: WILSON MIDDLE SCHOOL

It's not uncommon for principals and coaches to wonder how to make the most out of their weekly planning sessions. This was the focus of an observation that I facilitated with a team of secondary principals and coaches in Council Bluffs, Iowa. The district had set the expectation for principals and coaches to meet on a weekly basis, but there were questions about how to leverage these conversations to directly impact student learning.

I worked with the director of secondary education to design an observation for fifteen coaches and principals, based on a coaching lab model in which a group observes a coaching conversation and then engages in a debriefing session to discuss the coaching practice, implications, and their questions.

The observation focused on Joel, the principal at Wilson Middle School. He was working hard to connect coaching and student learning, and we observed one of his weekly conversations with the coaches in his school.

As you read through the conversation, see if you can identify the ways in which Joel creates a high-accountability and high-support system. How does he connect the dots between coaching and student learning?

### The Observation

Joel began by framing what he hoped to get out of the planning session. He said, "There is one literacy team that we need to discuss. It's the team you've been working with, and I'm noticing a divide among the four teachers. We are seeing a lot of growth in some areas. For example, Kelsey and Holly are having some great conversations about the thinking they expect their students to do. I know you've been working with them on their instruction, and I'm glad to see the progress. I'd like to see them spending more time looking at student work, maybe in terms of their next unit on literacy analysis. What do you think?" Tera and Casey agreed that they have seen a lot of progress and liked the idea of introducing student work into their conversations with the teachers.

Joel continued, "That said, I'm concerned about the other teachers on the team. I've noticed that Rick and Denise are struggling. During my last walk-through, I heard them telling the students they were focusing on analysis and evaluation when they were really targeting lower-level skills. When I talked with them about it, they didn't seem to understand the difference. I also noticed that during yesterday's professional development session, they sat back and let Kelsey and Holly do all of the thinking for them. There was also some nonverbal disengagement. I guess I'm wondering if you are seeing the same thing."

Tera replied, "When I've worked with them recently, they seem to be unsure of how higher-order thinking fits into their language arts curriculum. They are a bit reluctant to adjust what they are already doing."

Joel nodded and replied, "Yesterday, I suggested that they do a coaching cycle. I thought it would be with Casey, since Tera is about to leave for maternity leave. They agreed and seemed to be willing. Rick asked if he could see some examples of what a coaching cycle looks like in other classrooms—maybe through videotaping or observations. I thought Casey's role would be to facilitate these conversations. But we also need to be sure to build in student work. Otherwise, we may not get at what matters . . . at least, that's my thinking."

Casey said, "We could do that. I know they get protective of their planning time. Would it be okay if our planning sessions took place during their PLC time?"

Joel agreed, "That's a great idea. This is a good use of PLC time, because it aligns with what we are trying to do and it won't require them to meet during an additional prep."

Casey solidified the plan by saying, "Okay, we'll focus on higher-order thinking, and that's where we'll pull in the student work. We'll also share some instructional strategies and provide examples for that through video or observations. I think I can do that."

Before they wrapped up, Joel brought up the professional development session that he had led the week prior. The topic had been working with teachers to identify practices for teaching higher-order thinking—a topic that some of the teachers were very familiar with and others were not.

The coaches often led the professional development sessions, but last week Joel decided to facilitate it. He shared that he didn't think it had gone as well as he had hoped it would. He said, "I noticed that the teachers seemed to be confused. I should have checked for understanding, just like we ask teachers to do. I missed the ball on that one. . . ."

They continued their discussion by brainstorming a few ideas for next week's professional development session. They closed with a clear understanding of what to do next and were glad that they'd be back together in a week to discuss their progress.

## The Debrief

As I listened to their conversation, I noticed how much ownership Joel took over setting the course for coaching and professional development in his school. He knew what was happening in classrooms and among teams and was able to problem solve in a way that honored what had been done while also moving each teacher forward. Now it was time to debrief with the other participants in the coaching lab.

In coaching labs, we organize the debriefing session around a series of rounds that are designed to move the observers from naming what they saw to thinking deeply about the implications for their own schools. In the first round, we identified

*(Continued)*

(Continued)

specific observations using the stems, "I saw . . ., I noticed . . ., I heard . . ." Here are some examples of what the principals and coaches shared:

- Joel asked for clarity from the coaches. He said, "Here's what I'm seeing in the classrooms. Are you seeing the same thing?"
- Everyone had the same understanding of higher-order thinking.
- Joel led the process for how teachers could participate in coaching.
- There was trust between Joel and the coaches.
- Joel set high expectations for the students, teachers, and coaches.
- Different strategies were introduced for different teachers.
- Joel reflected honestly about his delivery of professional development.
- There was an attitude that if something wasn't in place, we could fix it.
- The coaches asked Joel clarifying questions about how to implement his vision.
- The coaches continually came back to how they could align coaching, professional development, and supervision.

In the second round, we discussed how the conversation between the principal and the coaches would impact student learning. The group identified the following observations:

- Using student work will help the teachers group students in new ways.
- Being in classrooms helps the principal decide what needs to happen to propel student learning.
- Whenever the principal or coaches gave an example, it was always rooted in what was happening in classrooms.
- The principal was pushing for a tighter connection to the students by using more student work during coaching sessions.
- The conversation emphasized that the teacher is also a learner and that coaching helps teachers get better at what they do every day in the classroom.
- We can't assume that teachers know everything at the same level and at the same time.

To wrap up, each group member identified his or her own next steps based on what was observed:

- I now understand that my relationship with the coach is different than my relationship with teachers.
- I need to set a goal to spend more time in classrooms.
- I need to have more conversations with teachers about how they are approaching their instruction.

- I need to define *quality* when it comes to teaching and learning.
- I will strive for specificity when working with the coach and teachers.
- I will take a more hands-on approach to professional development.

Principals are learners too, and they often need strategies for leading a coaching effort. They rarely (if ever) get to observe their colleagues in action, so I expected that they would want to know more about Joel's strategies for leadership.

One of his colleagues asked why he chose to facilitate the professional development. Joel explained that he knew that the session would be challenging, so he decided to lead it himself. He said, "If someone is going to stumble, I want to be that person, because I want to set up my coaches for success." There was no question whether Joel was leading the coaching effort.

I've been facilitating coaching labs for several years, and this one was one of the most meaningful that I've experienced. Witnessing a group of isolated school leaders coming together to learn from a colleague is an unbelievably rare event in our school systems. Other than their weekly administrative meetings, principals rarely are treated as learners, and this group made the most of their afternoon together.

## PRINCIPAL AND COACH ROLES

We can't drop a coach in a school, cross our fingers, and hope that something will come of it. We have to be a bit more strategic than that. We have to understand how to leverage the leadership of the principal with the ongoing support that can be provided by a coach. If we play our cards right, teachers will come to understand, with clarity, what is expected of them. And they will also come to understand that they will be supported and held accountable for making that happen. So far, this chapter has addressed the role of accountability, data, and principal/coach collaboration in making that happen. Figure 5.3 in Tools and Techniques provides a comprehensive look at how these factors come together to create a system that is rich in both accountability and support.

## TOOLS AND TECHNIQUES

The following protocol guided the observation of Joel and his team. The rounds are designed to move the conversation from an objective level of "I saw . . . , I noticed . . . , I heard . . ." to a place in which the participants identify and consider the implications of what they saw in terms of their

3   School Leadership and Coach Collaboration

| Roles | |
|---|---|
| **School Leadership** | **Coach** |
| Sets high expectations for teacher and student learning. | Provides support to teachers so they can meet the expectations that have been established by the school leadership. |
| Holds teachers accountable for meeting the needs of the students. | Organizes coaching so that it aligns with the accountability measures that are in place. |
| Establishes a vision and sets priorities for how to move student learning forward. | Prioritizes work that has the most potential to impact student learning. |
| Makes strategic use of the coach to move teacher learning forward. | Articulates his or her role as a coach and engages teachers in the coaching process. |
| Leads the decision making about the scope and breadth of the content that is taught. | Helps teachers design instruction that aligns with expectations about the content that is being taught. |
| Knows what high-quality instruction looks like and sets the expectation that this is the norm throughout the school. | Skillfully supports teachers to implement high-quality instruction. |
| Is aware of situations when students are underperforming and works to address the issue. | Works with teachers across all levels of performance. |
| Leads data-driven conversations with teachers and the coach. | Participates in data-driven conversations with teachers and the principal. |
| Spends time in classrooms and provides teachers with feedback as a result of the observations. | Spends time in classrooms to support the delivery of effective instruction. |
| Creates the structure, time, and expectations that allow teachers to collaborate with each other and the coach. | Designs and facilitates collaboration among teachers. |

own schools. We organized the rounds by moving around the table so that we could hear from everyone in the room. In closing, participants were provided with an opportunity for open-ended discussion and problem solving (Figure 5.4).

**Figure 5.4** Coaching Lab Protocol

**Prebrief**

The host of the coaching lab provides the context and focus for the observation. Typically, the observation is framed around a dilemma that has been brought up or goal that the coach or principal are working toward. By framing the observation around a dilemma or goal, the host provides the observers with the opportunity to support their colleague and also to reflect on their own work with teachers.

**Observation**

The group observes a coaching conversation as it happens. While observing, participants take notes that will inform the debriefing session. Often, coaching labs focus on one of the following areas:

- Planning session with a teacher or team of teachers
- Planning session with the principal
- Small-group collaboration or PLCs
- Co-teaching or modeling in the classroom
- Observing a teacher to provide feedback

**Debrief**

The debriefing session is guided by the following rounds. A whip-around format in which each observer has a turn to share is used. At the end of each round, the facilitator synthesizes the key points from the round. The lab host listens and takes notes in order to respond during the fourth round.

*Round 1: Coaching Observations*

What did you see, notice, or hear during the coaching conversation?

*Round 2: Connection to Student Learning*

How will student learning be influenced by the coaching conversation?

*Round 3: Questions*

What questions do you have for the lab host?

*Round 4: Lab Host Responds*

How would the lab host like to respond to what was shared?

*Round 5: Group Reflection and Next Steps*

What were the implications of what you observed? What is your next step for your work with teachers?

## IN SUMMARY

Getting clear about the different roles for the coach and principal creates conditions for coaches to do their best work. Without this clarity, the impact of coaching is jeopardized. And when coaching is jeopardized, teacher and student learning are jeopardized as well.

The lives of schools leaders can be hectic and overwhelming. And while this chapter makes the argument that coaching requires leadership, my hope is that the work doesn't have to be a lonely or overwhelming affair. There are some important distinctions between the role of the coach and the role of the school leader. But even with these differences, their collaboration can be designed to play the same tune. By crafting a plan that includes high levels of accountability and support, learning will progress for both the teachers and the students.

# 6 Designing a School Culture That's About Student Learning

Issues around climate and culture stubbornly persist in many of our secondary schools. And since culture is a powerful force, we can't have an honest conversation about coaching without addressing it as well.

To explore school culture from all angles, this chapter will be divided in two sections. The first will look at how school leaders can work to design a school culture that's about student learning. The second will introduce a set of coaching practices to be applied within a culture of learning. By tackling school culture from the perspectives of design and application, there will be increased clarity around how the two sides work together to move teaching and learning forward.

## Part I: Designing a Student-Centered School Culture

### THE "NO OPT OUT" SCHOOL CULTURE

Setting high expectations for student learning and then holding teachers accountable for reaching those expectations creates a high-performance culture for both the students and teachers. Doug Lemov (2010) tackles this in his book *Teach Like a Champion: 49 Techniques That Put Students on the Path to College* when he writes, "One consistent finding of academic research is that high expectations are the most reliable driver of high student achievement, even in students who do not have a history of successful achievement" (p. 30).

One of Lemov's strategies for setting high academic expectations is what he refers to as *no opt out*. He explains that teachers who use a no opt out model of instruction are vigilant in maintaining the expectation that it's not okay not to try. He writes, "Everybody learns in a high-performing classroom, and the expectations are high even for students who don't yet have high expectations for themselves" (p. 28).

This begs the question of how we might establish a culture of high expectations for teachers as well. The no opt out philosophy would serve us well in creating a shared culture that is focused on doing what's best for each and every student, therefore eliminating the possibility that teachers are doing things as they have been done without absolute certainty that the things they are doing are moving the students to meet or exceed the standards. It also removes the option for some teachers to engage in coaching while others sit on the sidelines. A no opt out school culture implies that *everyone* engages in the hard work of doing what's best for the students.

## WHAT ABOUT BUY-IN?

Chapter 2 introduced the differences between invitational and assigned coaching and suggested that rather than asking the question of how to get teachers to buy in, we should be thinking about crafting a culture that sets an expectation around teacher participation. We can't sit back and wait for buy-in to happen; we have to set expectations for how teachers will engage. Bambrick-Santoyo (2010) writes, "The best initiatives in schools—and elsewhere—do not require buy-in, they create it" (p. 107).

Creating buy-in requires a skilled leader who understands how to get teachers to participate honestly in improvement efforts. Documenting how students are learning and how coaching led us there creates buy-in by providing a rationale for why the work is necessary and important.

Data also plays a role in establishing buy-in. In some cases, data has the potential to write a narrative for what is (or isn't) happening in terms of student learning. When data is valid and holds meaning for teachers, it can create a compelling argument that something must be done. The reverse can also be true. When data feels irrelevant or misguided, it can do just the opposite: It undermines buy-in. The assessments we use to drive our decision making had better paint a clear picture regarding how student performance is measuring up to the standards. And if the data isn't able to tell this story, then it's time to look for something else.

In the heat of an improvement effort, it is easy to slip into the mindset of "making people do things." We forget to ask for input from the school community and tend to avoid the difficult conversations that come with anything that's new or different. The danger is that avoidance creates distrust, and distrust creates negativity.

Seeking the opinions of teacher leaders provides invaluable insight into how school reforms, a new curriculum or program, and other initiatives are being translated into the classroom on a daily basis. We can create buy-in by believing in teachers, trusting their judgment, and asking for their opinions.

## QUALITIES OF A SCHOOL THAT MAINTAINS A CULTURE OF LEARNING

Crafting a culture of learning can be described as everything from a long, hard slog to guerilla warfare. Nobody would suggest that it's easy, but in spite of its grueling nature, there are many examples of schools that have tackled the mess of culture to create environments that are wholly oriented around teaching and learning.

Unfortunately, there are also many schools that operate based on what's best for the teachers. And there are others that lack the knowledge or energy that is required to create and sustain a culture of learning. To move beyond these sticking points, it is important to understand what's possible by unpacking the qualities of a school with an established culture of learning:

- School leaders view themselves as learners.
- School leaders understand and push for effective instruction.
- Coaching and professional development are designed around specific and measurable goals for student learning.
- Formative and interim assessments are used to track student learning.
- Analysis of student work guides the decision making.
- The needs of the system are secondary to a focus on student learning.
- Time within the school day is provided for teachers to reflect as individuals, in small groups, or with a coach.
- There is a climate of trust where it is okay to make mistakes during the learning process.

# DEVELOPING SYSTEMS TO SUPPORT TEACHER LEARNING

The systems that we create for teacher learning have the potential to reinforce a culture of learning and high expectations. Systems that are student centered provide teachers with a clear-eyed focus on the students' performance. This is a departure from more traditional models of professional development in which we train teachers to use specific practices or programs with their students; a student-centered approach to professional development puts the students' needs front-and-center (Figure 6.1).

**Figure 6.1** A Student-Centered Framework for Professional Development

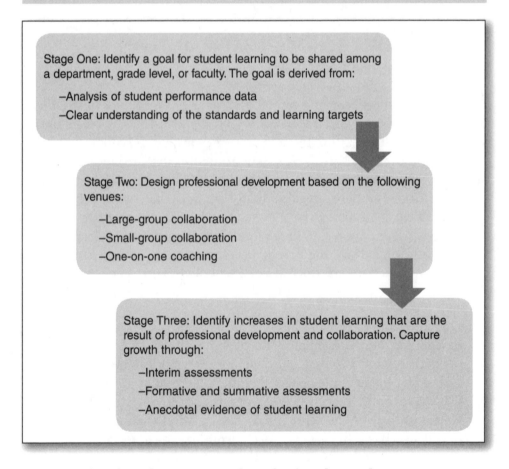

Stage One: Identify a goal for student learning to be shared among a department, grade level, or faculty. The goal is derived from:

–Analysis of student performance data
–Clear understanding of the standards and learning targets

Stage Two: Design professional development based on the following venues:

–Large-group collaboration
–Small-group collaboration
–One-on-one coaching

Stage Three: Identify increases in student learning that are the result of professional development and collaboration. Capture growth through:

–Interim assessments
–Formative and summative assessments
–Anecdotal evidence of student learning

## An Example of Student-Centered Professional Development

The teachers at Arrupe Jesuit High School noticed that their students were more capable when it came to writing personal narratives than writing in the content areas. It was a gap that presented itself through the data, and it was hard to ignore. The teachers knew they had to do something to address this problem, because content-area writing was emphasized in the standards and was something the students would need to do when they reached college. Content-area writing became their goal for student learning.

The coach and principal worked together to design a framework for the teachers to meet as a full faculty, in small groups, and in one-on-one coaching. In these groups, they studied best practices for teaching writing in the content areas, analyzed student work, collaboratively planned instruction, and continually looked at the data.

The principal made it clear that buying in wasn't an option. That said, the teachers' input was valued, and they were provided with many choices about how to learn together. Figure 6.2 illustrates their framework for professional development.

**Figure 6.2** Three Venues of Professional Development

**Large-Group Sessions** include the full faculty, combined departments, or teams. In the early stages, these sessions involve the use of data to set clear and measurable goals for students. When a goal is in place, the faculty shifts in order to research and develop teaching practices that will accomplish the goal. Practices for this venue include

- data analysis to identify a goal for student learning;
- investigation of resources such as teaching practices, programs, or curriculum that will directly target the students' needs; and
- use of professional development strategies such as classroom observations, professional reading, PLCs, or other forms of discussion to develop the teachers' abilities to address the students' needs in the classroom.

**Small-Group Sessions** include smaller teams, such as grade levels or departments. At this stage, teams move through a continuous loop of analysis of student data and designing instruction. Practices for this venue include

- the use of data teams to continually analyze student progress;
- coaching cycles with teams of teachers;
- protocol-based discussions to develop and share teaching practices that align with the goal for student learning; and
- classroom-based observations, further study, and collaborative planning to refine the teaching practice.

**One-on-One** coaching includes individuals or pairs of teachers. This venue is individualized and focuses on the needs of specific students and teachers. Practices for this venue include

- continual collaborative analysis of student evidence or data;
- coaching that may include demonstration teaching, co-teaching, or observation by the coach; and
- ongoing planning conversations by the coach and teacher(s).

A student-centered framework for professional development focuses on capturing student growth based on the goal that the teachers set for them. We can't neglect this part of the process, because it reminds teachers of why they are there in the first place. It is so easy to jump ahead and get wrapped up in what has to happen next. But taking the time to analyze both formal and informal assessment data shows teachers what has been accomplished and also presents many opportunities for where to go next. In fact, it just might lead to a new goal for student learning and will begin the process all over again.

The guiding questions in Figure 6.3 support the process of planning professional development that is student centered.

**Figure 6.3**  Guiding Questions for Planning Student-Centered Professional Development

- What data will we use to inform our decision making?
- How will we analyze the data to determine a professional development focus?
- How will we build ownership among the teachers as they engage in the process?
- What student work or assessment data will we use to measure progress?
- How will we provide support to teachers?
- How long do we think it will take to reach our goal?
- How will we measure the impact of the professional development on the students?
- How will the principal, coach, and leadership team collaborate?

## DEALING WITH DIFFERING BELIEFS

Chapter 5 introduced a vision for creating schools with high levels of accountability and support—a vision that has broad-ranging implications for the culture and climate of a school. When teachers understand what is expected of them, they perform at higher levels. And when the expectations aren't clear or are too low, student performance is jeopardized.

When designing a culture of learning, we have to be prepared to deal with teachers who have differing beliefs and expectations about what the students can or cannot do. DuFour, Eaker, and DuFour (2005) write,

Substantive and lasting change will ultimately require a transformation of culture—the beliefs, assumptions, expectations, and habits that constitute the norm for the people throughout the organization. Principals and teachers can be placed in new structures and go through the motions of new practices, but unless they eventually develop new competencies and new commitments that lead to true school reculturing, they will continue to be under the inexorable pull of their traditional practices and the assumptions that drive them. (p. 11)

Anthony Muhammad (2009) identifies a *war of paradigms* that includes four groups of teachers who have differing and often conflicting visions and beliefs. It is not in our best interest to ignore or try to work around the teachers whose beliefs are in conflict with our own. We have to understand who they are, what their beliefs are, and why they believe what they do. Muhammad's research indicates that there are four distinct groups in most school communities:

- The Believers—Believers hold high expectations for their students and believe that these expectations can be achieved. For the most part, they have been practicing teachers for more than three years, and as Muhammad writes, "They have made a decision to accept a student-centered paradigm as their primary mode of operation, regardless of outside opposition" (p. 31).
- The Tweeners—Tweeners are newer to the school culture and may be influenced by either the Believers or the negative teachers on staff. For the most part, Tweeners are eager to please, compliant, and want to do what's best for their students, though they may not be quite sure what that is.
- The Survivors—Survivors are a specific, and small, population of teachers who are unhappy as educators. They are unlikely to fully engage in efforts around school improvement, because they don't have the energy or interest to take on these types of challenges.
- The Fundamentalists—Fundamentalists are firmly rooted in a single definition of *schooling* and expect any necessary adjustments to be made by the students rather than by the teachers. Muhammad describes Fundamentalists as "staff members who are not only opposed to change, but organize to resist and thwart any change initiative. They can wield tremendous political power and are a major obstacle in implementing meaningful school reform. They actively work against the Believers" (p. 29).

If we want to truly effect change, every member of a school community must join in the effort to elevate our expectations for students and ward off the negativism and hostility that some teachers bring to our school communities. Principals can set the tone that the students' needs come before the teachers' personal beliefs. Coaches can build capacity throughout the school. And teachers can ban together in an effort to shift the school culture toward one that believes in students.

*[handwritten margin note: Interesting... these dynamics are a great read]*

## Part II: Coaching Within a Culture of Learning

Coaches live in a no-man's-land between the administration and the teachers. This often presents a fair amount of stress and uncertainty for coaches. Is their role to hold teachers accountable? Are they there to provide resources in a nonthreatening way? Where does their influence begin and end? Where is their place within the school culture?

In schools where a culture of learning has been established, these questions are far less pressing. Teachers understand that they are expected to continually push the envelope of both their learning and the learning of their students, and coaches understand their role in making this happen. Their work becomes not only more meaningful but easier, because it rests within a culture of learning.

## CULTURE AND CONFIDENTIALITY

The question of confidentiality is a tricky one. I've worked with principals who expect a coach to maintain complete confidentiality in order to promote trust among the teachers. I've also worked with principals who believe that high levels of confidentiality work against creating a culture of openness and learning. They feel that teachers are part of a broader system and shouldn't operate behind closed doors or behind a shroud of confidentiality.

In my experience, if the coach and principal wish to head in the same direction, they'd better get on the same page regarding the degree to which coaching should remain confidential. The following guiding questions will help the coach and principal understand how to navigate through issues related to culture and confidentiality (Figure 6.4).

**Figure 6.4**  Guiding Questions Regarding Confidentiality and Coaching

- How will the coach build trust with teachers?
- How will the school leader support the trust-building process?
- How will the coach and school leader share specific information about teachers?
- How will data be used by the school leader and coach to get specific about strategies for improving student learning?
- How often, and in what ways, will the principal spend time in classrooms to get a personal perspective of how things are going?
- What coaching notes and documentation will be shared with the principal?
- What will remain confidential between the teacher and coach?

Before we leave the subject of confidentiality, it's important to note that an essential quality for coaches is to maintain absolute professionalism when it comes to their work with teachers. Teachers have to understand that they aren't being judged and that their weaknesses aren't being broadcast to others. A culture of learning requires that teachers feel comfortable taking risks. And a coach who criticizes or judges teachers undermines learning among teachers and students.

## FEEDBACK THAT CONTRIBUTES TO A CULTURE OF LEARNING

The ability for teachers to learn from feedback, and for coaches to effectively provide feedback, is greatly impacted by the school culture. In schools with a learning orientation, teachers understand the important role that feedback plays. In other schools, a coach may never get the opportunity to provide the teachers with the feedback they need to meet their students' needs.

Here's the conundrum: Teachers can't learn without feedback. But providing feedback to colleagues can feel exceedingly uncomfortable for many coaches. What's a coach to do?

I was recently in a situation where I was learning something new and challenging—a telemark ski lesson. Telemark skiing is also known as *free heel skiing*, because the skier's heel isn't connected to the ski, which means the turn is exactly opposite of regular skiing. I've skied my whole life and can hold my own on most slopes, but since I decided to learn how to telemark, I had to learn how to ski all over again. Yep, I was back on the bunny slope.

So I signed up for a one-day clinic with an experienced instructor. While the instructor did a great job explaining the technical aspects of the sport, he used generic terms and didn't personalize his instruction to any of the eight students in the class. While we were technically at the same level, we were all experiencing our own (and very different) challenges as we tried to get down the hill in one piece.

I was dying for feedback. I wanted to know if I was using the proper technique, and if I wasn't, I wanted to know what I should be doing differently. Otherwise, I knew that the whole day of instruction was a waste of time and energy. As the day progressed, I came to realize that the instructor was not planning to provide specific feedback to anyone in the class. Instead, he continued to re-explain the same information over and over again and left it up to us to figure out how to actually implement what we were supposed to be implementing. I left the class feeling frustrated, having clearly missed an opportunity to learn.

The fact that I had made the choice to learn something new is in direct correlation with my desire to improve and my need for feedback. This isn't always the case for teachers—they don't always get to choose the learning that they are expected to be doing. So it is up to the coach to create opportunities for teachers to have choice and ownership about the feedback they receive. Framing coaching around a goal for student learning is one way to make new learning relevant for teachers. Coaching becomes less personal, because it is about what we need to do to move the student learning forward, and therefore, the feedback will be more readily accepted.

The quality of feedback increases with specificity, and specificity requires the provider of the feedback to be present in all that is going on around them. In a busy classroom, this means that the coach or teacher notes the instruction, the student behaviors, how the students are doing as learners, and any other bits of information that seem to fly by at Mach 10 speed.

I find that I can get more specific in providing feedback when I know a few things. First, I need to know the teacher's goals for student learning. If I focus my feedback on how the students are doing in relationship to the teachers' goals, feedback becomes less touchy. When I'm in the classroom, the process I use to take notes is focused on the students in order to create a platform for feedback that is nonthreatening to teachers. On my notes, I list the goals for student learning (or learning targets), and then I note evidence of how the students are doing in relationship to the teachers' goal (Figure 6.5).

**Figure 6.5** Student-Centered Coaching Notes

**Goals for Student Learning (Learning Targets):**

**Evidence of Student Learning:**

At times, teachers request feedback that is specific to their instruction rather than to their students' learning. When this is the case, feedback becomes personal because it is about what the teacher did during the lesson. Rather than making assumptions about what feedback is desired by a teacher, I like to find out what the teachers' comfort zone is when it comes to feedback. I often ask, "Do you like your feedback hot, medium, or cold?" When teachers respond with *hot*, I know that they are eager for a lot of specific feedback, much like I desired during my ski lesson. A response of *medium* or *cold* indicates that a teacher may feel a bit more tentative and is a cue to infuse feedback in a slow and deliberate manner so as not to overwhelm the teacher.

The natural place to talk about this is when I set agreements with the teacher. As soon as expectations have been set regarding feedback, both the coach and teacher will be more comfortable having honest conversations with each other. I use the following note-taking tool when the teachers request feedback about their instruction so that I stay true to what they feel they need (Figure 6.6).

Providing relevant and specific feedback is a skill that I am constantly working to improve. Just yesterday, I was shadowing a coach, and she asked me for feedback. After an initial feeling of discomfort, I reread my notes, thought about the goals she had set, and began a conversation about how she could take her work to the next level. As a learner, she deserved that.

## USING VIDEO AS A SOURCE OF FEEDBACK

Most athletic coaches will tell you how much they depend on video as a source of feedback for their athletes. Video provides athletes with the ability to look closely at their performance to determine what they are doing well and what should be changed the next time they take to the field, court, or slopes. All the explanation in the world can't make up for seeing yourself in action.

The use of video is becoming more common in today's landscape of improving teacher effectiveness. School districts are using cameras that capture 360-degree views of classrooms. Others have systems in which a coach can remotely observe teachers and provide input through earpieces. And most coaches have the technology to videotape teachers at any given moment through portable cameras or iPads.

With so many choices regarding technology, many schools are wondering how to tap into it in a way that contributes to, rather than detracts from, the school culture. There is no question that videotaping teachers can be a touchy subject. I know this from personal experience. While I am

**Figure 6.6** Tool for Organizing Feedback About Classroom Instruction

| Name: <br> Date: | Type of Feedback (circle): | Hot | Medium | Cold |
|---|---|---|---|---|
| **Goals for Student Learning:** | | | | |
| **Goals for Instruction:** | | | | |
| **+ What's Working?** | | | | |
| **Δ What Might I Change?** | | | | |

completely comfortable speaking in front of large groups of people, I find watching myself on video to be an absolutely painful experience. I have an innate discomfort seeing myself on video, and I'm sure that many other teachers do as well.

I am regularly asked how coaches can use video in their coaching. The idea of filming and then debriefing a lesson is appealing when budgets are tight, because we can provide models of instruction with very little expense. And while I agree that budget is a factor, video has its limitations.

When the focus is teacher centered and about the instructional practices (or delivery) of the instruction, then viewers can often get something out of watching a teacher deliver a lesson. They can watch a teacher in action, note the instructional practices, and then improve upon them the next time around.

The challenge comes in when the focus is on both the instruction and the student learning. When I am in classrooms, I am not only watching a lesson, I am trying to capture evidence of what the students are doing as learners and how it relates back to the learning targets. I get close, listen to their conversations, and take notes about what they are saying and doing. It's easy to set up a camera in a classroom to capture the teaching, but it is far more challenging to capture student learning as it relates to the teaching that takes place. Short of bringing in a crew of cameras and providing each student with a microphone, I'm not sure how to accomplish this on video. So for now, I feel comfortable using video when instructional practice is the focus. But when analyzing student learning is the goal, I find that I need to be in the classroom to understand the learning that is taking place.

## A CASE IN POINT: BELIEFS AT ARRUPE JESUIT HIGH SCHOOL

Edgar Schein (1994) culture as "the deeper level of *basic assumptions* and *beliefs* that are shared by members of an organization, that operate unconsciously, and that define in a basic 'taking-for-granted' fashion an organization's view of itself and its environment [italics in original]" (p. 41). Coming to some form of an agreement about our most basic beliefs and assumptions is a vital step for building a school culture that's about student learning. We simply can't afford to operate unconsciously but instead must take careful steps to dictate the terms of the culture that we would like to create.

As a no opt out school culture, Arrupe Jesuit High School operates from a set of core beliefs that serve as drivers of the school culture. Their beliefs don't live in the background but instead are front-and-center to the decision making by administrators, coaches, and teachers. They were created collaboratively and are continually refined over time (Figure 6.7). As you read through their beliefs, you will notice that they have four important qualities:

1. They are student centered.

2. They respect the challenges that teachers face as they strive to meet the needs of *all* students.

*(Continued)*

(Continued)

3. They set the expectation that best practices drive teaching and learning.

4. They are actionable and measurable.

**Figure 6.7** Arrupe Jesuit's Beliefs About Teaching and Learning

- Students are at the center of our decision making. Their identities, assets, needs, and goals lead to their success in college and in life.
- Effective teaching and learning results from planning—lots of planning. Teachers plan for understanding and anticipate confusion.
- Students need to do the work. Each student needs to think, read, write, problem solve, experiment, investigate, research, debate, question, wonder, analyze, organize, doubt, and so on. We handicap them by doing it for them!
- Students learn by doing, not by sitting and getting. Their voices matter as much as—if not more than—ours. This requires planning and humility.
- Less is more when it comes to *uncovering* and *discovering* content. *Covering* content only frustrates the learner and undermines the learning.
- Great teaching is the product of using effective practices. It's not magic; it's learned and practiced.
- We have enormous influence over student learning. Each minute with us counts, and we have no time to waste.
- No one has it all figured out. There is no perfect lesson, perfect day, perfect student, or perfect teacher.
- Teaching is hard work; therefore, it is critical that we collaborate by sharing our strengths, our dilemmas, our successes, and our failures.

The Tools and Techniques section of this chapter includes a set of benchmarks that can be used to assess the culture of your own school. It is meant to provide direction for how to tackle the challenges related to creating a student-centered school culture. However, as you reflect on your own school, you may find that crafting a set of beliefs for student and teacher learning is your first step in this journey. If this is the case, Arrupe Jesuit's beliefs might just provide the inspiration you are looking for.

## TOOLS AND TECHNIQUES

### Assessing Your School Culture

The following benchmarks are designed for a faculty to use to self-assess and set goals related to school culture. Rather than tackling everything at once, it is often necessary for a school to identify one area to work toward at a time. As I mentioned earlier in this chapter, working through issues of climate and culture can be a long, hard slog, and choosing one area to tackle at a time may be the only way to survive.

Benchmark I: Members of the school community hold one another accountable through open, honest, and trusting dialogue.

- The leadership understands the challenges of teaching but also encourages efforts at improvement.
- Experimentation is encouraged and shared.
- Mistakes are viewed as part of the learning process.
- Teachers are able to challenge the school leadership and vice versa.
- Dialogue is at the collegial level.

Benchmark II: Members of the school community are supported through student-centered coaching.

- Coaching provides teachers with ongoing and needs-based support.
- Teachers determine a student-centered focus for coaching.
- Coaching is driven by student evidence and assessment data.

Benchmark III: A shared set of beliefs drives the teaching and learning in the school.

- Creating a set of beliefs is a collaborative process.
- The beliefs encompass best practices for teaching and learning.
- The beliefs are student centered.
- The beliefs are actionable and measurable.

Benchmark IV: Professional development is designed to support teacher and student learning.

- The Three Venues (large group, small group, one-on-one) are used to organize professional development.
- There is a clear and well-understood goal for teacher learning.
- The goal for teacher learning comes from data or student work.
- The goal for teacher learning is determined by the faculty to ensure that there is a sense of shared ownership for the work.

Benchmark V: Collaboration among the principal, teachers, and coach is grounded in student work.

- Conversations about teaching and learning are shaped by student work.

- Well-designed processes and protocols guide the use of student work.
- Teachers are held accountable to apply what is learned during collaboration.

Benchmark VI: Focused and rigorous collaboration takes place on a consistent basis.

- Time is allocated for teacher collaboration.
- Skilled facilitator(s) manage the collaboration process.
- Teachers understand how to collaborate effectively.
- There is a broad array of collaboration processes in use (i.e., protocols, norms, etc.).

Benchmark VII: Learning is expected. Members of the school community are provided with the resources they need to engage in learning. The school leader and coach view themselves as learners.

- The school leadership and coach understand that teachers are not "fixed" but rather are encouraged to be active participants in the learning process.
- The school leadership and coach understand how to create systems for supporting teacher learning.

Benchmark VIII: Members of the school community support and encourage one another both publicly and privately.

- Members of the school community are not adversarial or competitive.
- The teachers, the principal, and the coach look for opportunities to share the successes of every colleague.
- There is a platform for sharing successes, whether in a faculty meeting, in a weekly bulletin, in grade level meetings, in department meetings, and so on.
- Certain teachers aren't favored over others. Rather, the successes of all teachers are shared.

Benchmark IX: Members of the school community observe one another for the purpose of sharing practices, asking questions, and considering teaching dilemmas.

- There is an established structure for learning labs (see Chapter 7).
- All teachers are provided with the opportunity to participate as hosts or observers in learning labs.
- A skilled facilitator manages the learning lab process.

## IN SUMMARY

Changing a school culture is no picnic. As Roland Barth (2007) puts it, "Probably the most important—and the most difficult—job of the school-based reformer is to change the prevailing culture of a school. The school's culture dictates, in no uncertain terms, 'the way we do things around here'" (p. 159). While the work isn't easy, we can't throw in the towel, because we know how intrinsic school culture is for creating conditions for learning.

Creating a no opt out culture with high expectations is paramount to our success. Paul Bambrick-Santoyo (2010) writes,

> Studies of high-achieving schools often talk about the influence of "culture" or "shared vision" in their success. The question to ask, however, is not whether high-achieving schools have a strong culture of high expectations—they universally do—but what were the drivers that created such a culture in each school? (p. 106)

My goal for this chapter has been to provide a comprehensive (yet realistic) vision regarding the importance, challenges, and necessary steps in creating a school culture that's about the performance of our students. Part I emphasized the role of the principal as the culture leader. Part II defined how a coach can work within the school and contribute to create a culture of learning.

Like anything else, culture needs to be tackled one step at a time. So whether you choose to use the benchmarks that were included in Tools and Techniques to identify a starting point or if you look to another source, the key is working from a clear set of beliefs about student learning and then designing structures for coaching and professional development that are based on what you believe is essential. Creating a no opt out school culture is a necessity because meeting the needs of all of our students requires each and every member of our school community.

# 7 Student-Centered Learning Labs

I t was a busy time of year for the teachers at West High School. The end of the school year was approaching, and Jen had been trying to schedule a learning lab since spring break. Jen was the literacy coach at West, and her role included creating opportunities for small groups of teachers to observe in each other's classrooms. A group of teachers had requested to participate in a learning lab before the year ended, and Jen wanted to make sure it happened.

Like many urban high schools, West had seen its fair share of school reforms and grant-funded initiatives. One of those projects involved the nonprofit I was working for at the time, the Public Education and Business Coalition (PEBC). PEBC provided professional development support to districts in and outside of Colorado. While serving as a project manager for the organization, I had heard about the learning labs at West and was hoping to see them in action. After a string of e-mails, Jen and I finally settled on a date—May 5th. At the time, neither of us realized that we had scheduled the observation for Cinco de Mayo, a lively day in Denver, CO.

## THREE GENERATIONS OF LEARNING LABS

Learning labs create a framework that allows teachers to get into each other's classroom for facilitated observations. While the overarching process for the labs has stayed consistent over the years (Figure 7.1), the observations have progressively become more data driven and student centered—an evolution that I like to refer to as *the three generations of learning labs.*

**Figure 7.1**   Learning Labs—The Process

- Prebrief
- Classroom-Based Observation
- Debrief

## The First Generation of Learning Labs—Model Classrooms

My first experience with learning labs was at the PEBC in the early 1990s. Their model for classroom-based observations was introduced in 1991 by staff developers Stephanie Harvey and Liz Stedem. Stephanie and Liz had just returned from observing in classrooms affiliated with Teachers' College in New York, and part of their visit included an observation in Judy Davis's classroom. They were struck by both the quality of the teaching and the observation process. When they returned to Denver, they began to design the PEBC Lab Network—a series of lab classrooms where teachers would observe, reflect upon, and then implement high-quality instruction. More than twenty years later, the PEBC Lab Network still provides these opportunities for teachers from within and outside of Colorado.

At the time, instructional practice was going through a dramatic shift toward an emphasis on deep thinking, comprehension, and problem solving. This work proved to be complex, and the PEBC Lab Network helped teachers see what the instruction looked like in highly effective classrooms, and created an experience that helped them learn to implement what they saw with their own students.

The process used by the PEBC was carefully planned, facilitated, and guided by the Protocol for Observations in Model Classrooms (see Figure 7.8 in Tools and Techniques at the end of this chapter). Since the protocol focused directly on how the teacher was going about the business of teaching, it was essential for the lab hosts to use current educational research to provide high-quality instruction. In other words, the lab hosts had to exemplify great teaching; otherwise, we ran the risk of bringing teachers to classrooms that may not be the most effective models. For that reason, we vetted lab teachers using the following criteria:

- Lab teachers demonstrate research-based teaching practices.
- Lab teachers design instruction that engages students.
- Lab teachers are capable of articulating their thinking with other teachers.

- Lab teachers set a positive tone in the classroom.
- Lab teachers are thoughtful and passionate about teaching and learning.
- Lab teachers participate in professional development and coaching on a regular basis.
- Lab teachers are confident and willing to host other teachers to observe in their classroom.

## The Second Generation of Learning Labs—Peer Learning Labs

A few years later, a principal at Lake Middle School in the Denver Public Schools approached the PEBC about designing learning labs that would promote the effective delivery of instruction, counteract a closed-door culture, and extend teacher collaboration. He didn't feel that model classrooms were an option, since he worried that they would further the divide among the teachers since certain teachers would be identified as effective while others wouldn't. This wouldn't bode well within his efforts at building a learning community within the school.

PEBC coaches Anne Patterson and Brooke O'Drobinak worked with the principal to develop peer learning labs that were built around a philosophy of bringing groups of teachers together to wrestle with the challenges they were facing in the classroom. Rather than focusing on the classrooms of teachers who had been identified as highly effective, peer learning labs were hosted by teachers who were willing to bring a dilemma or focus question to work through with a small group of colleagues. It didn't take long for Anne and Brooke to realize that by inserting a question to guide the observation, the process became more collegial and inclusive because it was based on learning more than on demonstration.

Word spread, and as more schools began implementing peer learning labs, it became apparent that many teachers needed help framing a focus question that was authentic, meaty, and would take their learning (and the learning of their colleagues) further. So we created the criteria shown in Figure 7.2 to help teachers craft a focus question to frame the observation.

Much like at Lake Middle School, West High School used a peer learning lab model that evolved from a philosophy of bringing teachers together for shared study and inquiry. The lab that I would be observing at West was hosted by a language arts teacher, and the observers included a drama teacher, a social studies teacher, and a teacher from the math department.

As the teachers, coach, and I gathered for the prebrief, the teachers were justifiably frazzled. There was an end-of-the-year theater production in the works, another teacher was dealing with discipline issues that had cropped

**Figure 7.2** Crafting a Focus Question

1. What's on your mind regarding your teaching practice?

2. What is challenging you as a teacher?

3. What have you been trying lately to improve student learning?

4. What is a teaching technique or tool that you are using and would like feedback on?

5. What questions do you have regarding your students' learning?

6. Fill in the blank: In what ways will my students . . . ?

up before school, and the vintage building was buzzing with excitement about Cinco de Mayo. A few minutes into the prebriefing session, we noticed smoke wafting through the classroom windows. When we investigated, we realized that it was coming from the park across the street where a group of students had gathered to show off their fireworks and lowriders. Jen and I panicked. Was it a mistake to pull the teachers out of their classrooms for professional development on a day like this? But when I looked around, I realized that the teachers weren't fazed in the least. In fact, they were completely focused on the task at hand—talking about their teaching practice and student learning.

We turned back to the protocol. Jen asked Roberto, the host teacher, to talk through what he was hoping to get from the experience. He shared that he was having some problems with the assigned texts for his grade level. While he liked the readings that were included—classics that most 11th graders should probably read—he was noticing that his students weren't engaged. He had been struggling with this for some time and thought it would be helpful to get some feedback from his fellow teachers.

For today's lesson, he planned to use a narrative poem written by a Latino author. It was gritty and written from the perspective of a teenage boy living in the arroyos of southern California. Roberto shared that he hoped that since his students had schema for many of the same issues, they would more readily connect with the text. The plan was to have the students read and annotate the text. Then they would discuss what they read in small groups, and he would assess both their engagement and comprehension. As we wrapped up the prebrief, he named the focus questions that would guide our observation: *In what ways will my students engage with the text? How will they engage during their small-group discussions? Will they comprehend what they read?*

Peer learning labs aren't based on modeling expertise. They are about creating opportunities for teachers to come together to unpack questions and challenges about their practice. Roberto was selected as the lab host not because he was an expert teacher but because he was willing to bring a dilemma to share with his colleagues. These are the types of teachers we look for when identifying a host for a peer learning lab:

- Teachers who are encountering dilemmas related to their students' learning
- Teachers who regularly question their practice
- Teachers who craft a focus question to frame the observation
- Teachers who participate in coaching and professional development on a regular basis
- Teachers who are willing to take risks in front of their peers
- Teachers who aren't afraid to learn with a group of colleagues

We sat off to the side as the students filed in. Roberto began the lesson by providing some background about the text and set his expectations for what the students would do as readers. The students grabbed their highlighters and started reading, completely unconcerned by the extra adults in the room who were hovering and frantically scribbling notes. We noted that there was no question that the students were engaged by what they read. We heard personal connections to the poem and groups who were in deep discussions about the author's intentions. Roberto seemed to have been correct in assuming that the text he used had the potential to make an enormous difference when it came to student engagement.

As we began the debriefing session, the teachers carefully named what they saw in terms of both student behavior and Roberto's instruction. Throughout the conversation, an array of profound, though-provoking, and sometimes intimidating questions were raised and discussed by the teachers. In my view, the most interesting part of the discussion was when they worked through the implications of what they had observed. Questions about using classical versus modern texts, the role of student choice, and what this means when the students face the state assessment were discussed. The teachers were doing just what we hoped they would do: they were grappling with the meaning behind what they had observed.

As one might imagine, bringing teachers together in this way requires a carefully facilitated process that takes the conversation to deep levels while also protecting the teacher from hurtful or inappropriate behavior. While the team that observed Roberto was ready to dive in and contribute, sometimes this isn't the case. To play it safe, Jen always uses a protocol during observations. (See Figure 7.9 in Tools and Techniques for the Protocol for Peer Learning Labs.)

## The Third Generation of Learning Labs—Student-Centered Learning Labs

Thanks to the work of the PEBC, learning labs have been making an enormous difference for Denver's teachers. Many who have participated share that this has been their only opportunity to observe another teacher. Others have cited seeing the practices in action as a linchpin for implementing them with their own students.

But I was still a bit unsettled. Since the observations focused so much on instruction, I felt that were missing opportunities to learn about our students and their learning. In some cases, like the lab at West, teachers naturally migrated toward talking about the students. But many other observations that I participated in never moved in that direction. It occurred to me that with a simple adjustment to the protocol, we could focus on both the student learning and the instruction.

At the time, I was working with coaches and teachers in the Edmonds School District, just outside of Seattle. We were in the process of designing a student-centered coaching model, so adjusting the way we facilitated classroom-based observations made sense.

Our first effort at creating a student-centered learning lab was with Nicole, a special education teacher of mathematics. We decided that observing in her classroom would be a perfect opportunity to adapt the process we had been using to put more of a spotlight on the students. To make this happen, we incorporated a set of goals, or learning targets, that were based on Nicole's expectations and the standards. By adding this piece, we were able to frame the observation around both the teaching *and* learning that was happening in Nicole's classroom.

To prepare for the observation, Nicole's coach and lab facilitator, Julia, met with her to craft a focus question and create the learning targets. Julia helped Nicole draft the following focus question: *In what ways does writing help support the students' thinking and understanding in math?* And after some discussion, they settled on the following learning targets to identify what Nicole hoped the students would do during the class period (Figure 7.3).

On the morning of the lab, Nicole began by briefing the visiting teachers about her focus question, the students, and the standards she was working toward. Then she shared the learning targets while Julia charted them for our group to refer to later. Julia pointed out that Nicole's goals made it clear what types of data we would be collecting during the observation. She also referred the teachers to the protocol they would be using so that everyone understood the role they would be playing while in Nicole's classroom (see Figure 7.10 in Tools and Techniques). Finally, Julia provided a note-taking sheet to help the visiting teachers capture both the

**Figure 7.3** Nicole's Learning Targets

- Students use their math journals to record and demonstrate their thinking.
- Students' math journals include the appropriate math vocabulary.
- Students solve problems in two ways and then communicate which way works best.
- Students' math journals show that they are using a system for checking their work.
- Students demonstrate cognitive rigor and stamina.
- Students work independently.
- Students share with and learn from peers.

student evidence and observations about the practices that Nicole used during the instruction (see Figure 7.7 in Tools and Techniques).

Introducing the learning targets added value to the lab process as a whole. It led the teachers to engage in a rich discussion about what the students should be doing as mathematicians at this point in the school year. Focusing more directly on student learning became an important conduit for bringing the teachers together to create a shared understanding around expectations for each student in the classroom.

As a result of the learning targets, the teachers had a clear understanding of the evidence they should be collecting during the observation. They busied themselves with moving around the classroom and noting what the students were doing throughout the class period. Watching the students this closely was a new way for the teachers to observe in someone else's classroom. While in other learning labs, they had noted what the teacher did; this time, they paid closer attention to the students.

As they observed, the teachers took careful notes to bring to the debriefing session. This created a conversation that was rich with specific student evidence, evidence that moved the teachers to discuss the broader implications of what they saw. Each observer left with a clear understanding of how Nicole's instruction moved the students toward the standards. In some cases, this challenged the teachers' thinking. In others, it reinforced practices the teachers were already using.

## COACHING AND FOLLOW-UP

There is no question that classroom-based observations are an important tool for professional development and coaching. They encourage a level of discussion that is difficult to reach outside of the classroom context, they provide teachers with a support system to solve problems related to teaching and learning, and they build a collaborative culture. However, we can't consider learning labs to be a random act of professional development. I was reminded of this during what became known as the "Cinco de Mayo Lab," when I asked the teachers what advice they had for other schools that were incorporating labs into their professional development framework. One of the teachers turned to me and said, "I find these labs to be incredibly useful. . . . In fact, I'd trade in every other type of professional development just to participate in learning labs." As a true believer in the power of observation, I was thrilled to hear this. Then I realized he wasn't finished: "But I also find it to be incredibly frustrating when there isn't any follow-up. We come up with all of these great ideas and questions, and then if nothing happens, we are left hanging." It was a gut check, and I realized that we had been so focused on creating and facilitating the labs that we had forgotten about follow-up. The irony is that for a coach, teachers asking for ongoing support is the stuff of dreams; so why hadn't we thought of that? Here are some ways for coaches to create a thoughtful system of follow-up to learning labs.

• During the observation, the coach charts the topics or questions that the teachers want to continue discussing in the future. Collaboration around these topics can occur during existing professional learning communities (PLCs), department meetings, or in cross-curricular teams.

• The coach listens and recognizes when an issue repeatedly presents itself in discussions. Then the coach works with the school leadership to design a big-picture system of support for the teachers. For example, as schools make the transition to the Common Core Standards, questions about implementation might crop up time and time again. Therefore, the coach may need to work with the principal to design a framework of support that includes learning labs, professional development, and coaching.

• The coach may chose to design a follow-up lab on the same topic but in another teacher's classroom. This way, the group can extend their thinking into a different context.

• The coach listens for openings for coaching cycles with individuals or teams of teachers. If an opening presents itself, the coach wastes no time getting these cycles up and running.

• As a follow-up to an observation, teachers may choose to videotape themselves and/or their students to share and discuss at a future date.

## WHICH TYPE OF LAB IS RIGHT FOR YOU?

Student-centered and peer learning labs are open, inclusive, and accessible for all teachers. They serve an important role in building a collegial school culture in which teachers think and learn alongside each other. Model classrooms offer an enormous amount of support in districts that are initiating a new instructional program or curriculum, because they provide teachers with opportunities to see what the new program or curriculum looks like in action and then go back and do the same thing in their classrooms. They are also particularly useful in districts that have a large population of new teachers, as they provide a large degree of scaffolding and support.

Student-centered and peer learning labs are designed at the school level and are managed and facilitated by a school-based coach. Designing a network of model classrooms is best managed at the district level simply because identifying teachers as "experts" can damage relationships and school culture. If the identification of model classrooms is handled by the district, then the school avoids these cultural pitfalls. The following criteria will help you consider which type of learning lab is the best fit for your school or district:

**Model classrooms are a good fit if you**

- have a large number of new teachers,
- have identified classrooms and teachers that model exemplary instruction,
- are implementing a new program or curriculum,
- have district-level personnel to manage the project,
- are less concerned with building a collegial culture, and
- can provide teachers with the necessary release time.

**Peer learning labs are a good fit if you**

- are interested in building a collegial culture;
- have school-level personnel, such as a coach, to manage the project;
- feel that there is enough trust among teachers to get the project up and running (if not, then building some basic level of collegiality might be a first step in the process); and
- can provide teachers with the necessary release time.

**Student-centered learning labs are a good fit if you**

- are interested in guiding teachers to use student evidence in their daily decision making;
- are interested in building a collegial culture;

- have school-level personnel, such as a coach, to manage the project;
- feel that there is enough trust among teachers to get the project up and running (if not, then building some basic level of collegiality might be a first step in the process); and
- can provide teachers with the necessary release time.

## A CASE IN POINT: LEARNING LABS AT
## ARRUPE JESUIT HIGH SCHOOL

The teachers at Arrupe Jesuit High School aren't treated as isolated individuals who are toiling away behind closed doors to teach their respective subject matter. Far from it. Arrupe has established a culture that is oriented around meeting the needs of the students by providing teachers with the support they need to get there.

In Chapter 2, you read about how the coach at Arrupe Jesuit designed her work based on goals that were set by the teachers in their faculty action plans. She didn't sit on the sidelines, waiting for teachers to opt in to coaching. The same goes for learning labs. When there is a shared goal for student learning, it often becomes the focus of a learning lab.

Arrupe Jesuit uses a student-centered model for learning labs that braids together the observation of instruction and student learning. The half-day labs are facilitated by Brooke O'Drobinak, the director of curriculum and instruction, and occur on a monthly basis.

Learning labs at Arrupe Jesuit include a group of three to five teachers. Sometimes they are from the same department or grade level, and other times, the lab may involve a mixed group of observers. In the planning phase of an observation, Brooke works with the teacher to draft a letter to the observers that explains the teachers' goals for student learning and instruction. Writing the letter helps the lab host articulate what he or she is after and how he or she hopes to get there. It also provides direction to the observing teachers regarding what they should be watching for while in the classroom.

### Norms for Observation

There is no question that observations make the greatest impact when they are guided by shared agreements and expectations. Arrupe Jesuit uses the following guidelines to ensure that the observations are a collegial experience that moves the teachers' thinking forward (Figure 7.4).

*(Continued)*

(Continued)

**Figure 7.4**  Arrupe Jesuit's Norms for Learning Labs

- Take a learning stance. Be ready to follow a focus question generated by the host or a question derived from something you are working on in your own classroom to anchor your observations. Expect to learn something new to enhance your own practice. This is your time to tend to your own learning.
- Honor the existing tone, structure, and community by limiting any side conversations, keeping distractions to a minimum, and making sure cell phones are off.
- Remember that you are an observer and researcher. It is not your turn to teach or worry about discipline concerns. Trust that the host teacher knows his or her students and is a professional.
- Stay close to the action. Get in close during a conference, or listen in to students talking. Move about the classroom and gain a new perspective.
- Enjoy this opportunity to learn alongside colleagues as you see the many ways research informs ongoing instruction.
- Record your observations and be responsible for bringing these notes back to help frame the debriefing session. The notes you take will provide evidence of things you *saw and heard* as we create an "Observations Chart" during the debrief. Plan to share a copy of your notes with the host teacher to support his or her learning as well. The following note-taking format will aid you in the collection of observational data:

| Evidence of Student Learning | Teacher Practice | Thoughts and Wonderings |
|---|---|---|
|  |  |  |

## TOOLS AND TECHNIQUES

If we are going to ask teachers to allow their colleagues into their classrooms to observe, we'd better make sure that we know how to facilitate the process. We can't assume that teachers have had this type of experience (as most haven't), so it falls upon the facilitator to create and follow a protocol and to be ready to intervene if the discussion heads off track. The following tips and scenarios are helpful tools for anyone who is facilitating learning labs (Figures 7.5 and 7.6).

### Note-Taking Tool

Putting a note-taking tool in the teachers' hands provides them with concrete direction about what type of evidence they should be collecting during the observation. The following note-taking tool provides teachers with a clear sense of their role during the observation (Figure 7.7).

**Figure 7.5** Guidelines for Facilitating Observations

**Before the Observation**

- Spend time in the classroom where the observation will take place so that you know how to best support the teacher and collect data to inform the discussion.
- Work with the host teacher to craft a focus question and learning targets that will propel the thinking of the group.
- Don't make teachers cover their own classes. Instead, create a plan to release teachers that won't cause undue stress.

**During the Observation**

- Always use a protocol.
- Don't hesitate to refer back to the norms for the observation.
- If a group member fails to follow the protocol, point out the purpose for each step in the process.
- Hone your skills at probing and paraphrasing—these are the two most useful skills for lab facilitators.
- Add insight to provide clarity and extend the thinking of the observers.

**After the Observation**

- Reflect on how the lab went to plan for the next one.
- If the protocol didn't feel right, revise it.
- If participants didn't contribute as you had hoped they would, create a plan to help them better understand their role the next time around.

**Figure 7.6** Facilitation Scenarios

**Selecting the Lab Host**

As the principal, you are excited about implementing learning labs at your school. It has been your dream for teachers to learn from one another, but you were never quite sure where to begin. Now that you have a clear process to follow, you are ready to get started.

To kick off the labs, you introduce the lab concept to your faculty and share that it isn't about observing "expert" teachers and that everyone is encouraged to be a lab host. After introducing the idea, you invite the teachers to contact the coach if they would be willing to host in the first round, which will take place in a few weeks.

As the days pass, you are happy to see that a few teachers are willing to host a learning lab. You aren't surprised by two of the teachers, because they are voracious learners who take advantage of every learning opportunity that comes their way. Then you receive an e-mail from a teacher who is a bit of a surprise. She wants to host a lab even though she rarely participates in professional development and tends to be a negative voice among the staff.

*You aren't sure how to proceed in a way that honors the integrity of the labs and also gets them off to a positive start. What do you do?*

*(Continued)*

**Figure 7.6** (Continued)

**Here's What I Would Do:**

- Set the expectation that before a lab occurs, the hosting teacher will engage in a coaching cycle. That way, the coach will have established a relationship with the teacher and will be able to build on the teachers' strengths.
- Set the expectation that teachers articulate why they would like to host a lab. What is their dilemma related to teaching and learning, and what they hope to get out of the process?
- Encourage a broad array of teachers to host labs and be okay with any teacher who chooses to participate. This sends the message that labs are inclusive, and it reinforces the expectation for everyone on the faculty to be reflective and responsive to their students' needs.

✳ ✳ ✳

**Encouraging Thoughtful Response and Note Taking**

You are a coach and your school has been working on implementing learning labs for two months. The first lab has arrived and you will facilitate a group of five observing teachers.

Everything seems to go well during the prebriefing session. The host teacher talks about his instruction and how he has collaborated with you for the last several weeks. He has written up a thoughtful focus question and a clear set of learning targets. As the lab facilitator, you explain the norms for the observation, such as the importance of taking notes that are specific to the focus questions, not talking to students or each other, and so on.

During the observation, you glance around to see that only two of the five observers are taking notes. The rest have planted themselves in chairs in the back of the room. You don't want to interrupt the instruction, so you let it go. But when the debriefing session begins, you ask the observers to share what they noticed in regards to the focus question. A few of the teachers begin stating observations that are disconnected and irrelevant to the focus question, while others contribute thoughtfully. At the end of the round, you reframe the focus question to try to refocus the group. The two teachers who took notes contribute with comments that are thoughtful and relevant, while the others continue to bring forth less-than-helpful responses.

*You are worried on behalf of the lab host. He has been very thoughtful in his preparation, and you feel his hard work isn't being respected. What do you do?*

**Here's What I Would Do:**

- Be patient. We all need time to learn how to support one another.
- At the end of the first round, I would remind teachers that what is shared should directly relate to the teachers' focus question.
- I would ask the observers to think back through what they observed and jot down some additional notes that relate to the focus question. I'd give them a few minutes to do this, so they are more prepared for the next round.
- I would refer back to the learning targets and ask teachers to use the stem, "Evidence I saw that related to the targets included . . ."
- After this reframing, I wouldn't hesitate to redo the first round so that the hosting teacher gets what he needs from the experience. I'd also point out the importance of taking notes so that teachers can serve their colleagues throughout the process.

**Figure 7.7** Note-Taking Tool for Student-Centered Labs

| Teacher: |
| --- |
| Facilitator: |
| Date: |

| | | |
| --- | --- | --- |
| **Learning Targets** | | |
| | **Student Evidence** | **Instructional Practices** |
| | | |
| **Next Steps for Instruction and Assessment** | | |
| **Lingering Questions and Support Needed** | | |

## Protocols for Learning Labs

The protocols shown in Figures 7.8, 7.9, and 7.10 are specific to observations in model classrooms, peer learning labs, and student-centered learning labs.

**Figure 7.8** Protocol for Observations in Model Classrooms

| | |
|---|---|
| Prebriefing Session (30 minutes) | • The lab host provides background about the instructional practices that will be modeled.<br>• Information is shared about the standards, materials, and students in the classroom.<br>• Participants are invited to ask clarifying questions.<br>• Participants identify why they are participating in the observation and what new learning they would like to walk away with.<br>• The facilitator reminds the group of the observation norms. |
| Observation (50–60 minutes) | Participants observe the instruction and take notes to share during the debriefing session. |
| Debriefing Session (45 minutes) | The group debriefs in the following rounds. Throughout each round, the facilitator ensures that the responses are specific and objective. Each round is done as a whip around so that the discussion moves from one person to the next. Participants may pass when it is their turn to speak.<br><br>*Round 1: Instructional Practices*<br><br>• The group describes the instruction they observed in a nonjudgmental manner.<br>• The facilitator summarizes and/or charts the round, capturing the important themes and ideas that emerged from the discussion.<br>• The lab host listens and takes notes for further discussion.<br><br>*Round 2: Questions About the Instruction*<br><br>• Participants ask the lab host questions related to what they observed.<br>• The lab host responds to the questions and shares his or her thoughts about next steps for the instruction.<br><br>*Round 3: Next Steps*<br><br>• Each group member states a next step for his or her own work. The facilitator takes notes for future follow-up and coaching. |

**Figure 7.9** Protocol for Peer Learning Labs

| Prebriefing Session (30 minutes) | • The lab host introduces the focus question that will frame the observation.<br>• The teacher may choose to share recent lessons or artifacts from the classroom (such as charts, student work, or other assessment data) that will help the teachers understand the classroom context.<br>• Participants are invited to ask clarifying questions to the host teacher.<br>• Participants identify why they are participating in the observation and what new learning they would like to walk away with.<br>• The facilitator reminds the group of the observation norms. |
|---|---|
| Observation (50–60 minutes) | During the observation, the participants take notes that are specific to the focus question. |
| Debriefing Session (45 minutes) | The group debriefs using the following rounds. Throughout each round, the facilitator ensures that the responses are specific, objective, and do not include feedback or suggestions. Each round is done as a whip around so that the discussion moves from one person to the next. Participants may pass when it is their turn to speak.<br><br>*Round 1: What Did You See?*<br><br>• The group describes what they saw during the observation in a·nonjudgmental manner.<br>• The facilitator summarizes and/or charts the round, capturing the important themes and ideas that emerged from the discussion.<br><br>*Round 2: What Was the Impact on Student Learning?*<br><br>• The group describes how the teaching impacted student learning.<br>• The facilitator summarizes and/or charts the round, capturing the important themes and ideas that emerged from the discussion.<br><br>*Round 3: Response From the Host*<br><br>• The lab host responds and shares his or her thoughts and next steps for instruction.<br><br>*Round 4: Next Steps*<br><br>• In a whip around, each group member states a next step in his or her own work. The facilitator takes notes for future follow-up and coaching. |

**Figure 7.10**  Protocol for Student-Centered Learning Labs

| | |
|---|---|
| Prebriefing Session (45 minutes) | • The lab host introduces the focus question that will frame the observation.<br>• The lab host may also choose to share recent lessons or artifacts from the classroom (such as charts, student work, or other assessment data) that will help the teachers understand the classroom context.<br>• The lab host shares a set of learning targets using the guiding question, What will it look like if the students are demonstrating the intended learning?<br>• Participants are invited to ask clarifying questions to the host teacher.<br>• Participants identify why they are participating in the observation and what new learning they would like to walk away with.<br>• The facilitator reminds the group of the observation norms. |
| Observation (50–60 minutes) | • The facilitator hangs the chart of learning targets in the classroom during the observation so that the teachers can refer to them when taking notes. During the observation, the participants take notes that are specific to the focus question and learning targets. |
| Debriefing Session (60 minutes) | The group debriefs in the following rounds. Throughout each round, the facilitator ensures that the responses are specific and objective and do not include feedback or suggestions. Each round is done as a whip around so that the discussion moves from one person to the next. Participants may pass when it is their turn to speak.<br><br>*Round 1: Student Evidence*<br><br>• What specific evidence can participants provide to the teacher regarding the focus question and learning targets? What did the group see the students doing that matched the teacher's goals?<br><br>*Round 2: Implications*<br><br>• What are the broader implications of what was observed?<br><br>*Round 3: Response From the Host*<br><br>• The teacher responds by thinking aloud about what was shared. How has the teacher's thinking changed? What is a future goal for instruction?<br><br>*Round 4: Next Steps*<br><br>• Each group member shares a next step for his or her instruction. The facilitator takes notes for future follow-up and coaching. |

While the protocols are quite similar, there are some key differences that are worth noting. For example, when observing in model classrooms, teachers are encouraged to question and probe the host in order to fully understand the practices that they observed. Such questioning is not a part of the peer learning lab process, because the host teacher is a peer who is sharing a teaching dilemma with a group of colleagues. Probing teachers in this type of lab could be interpreted as a threat or criticism and may compromise the process, although this might be more common in schools that have been engaged in learning labs for a while and have developed a high level of trust.

Another key difference that was noted earlier in this chapter is identifying the learning targets during the prebriefing portion of a student-centered learning lab. Adding this feature immediately grounds the conversation in student evidence and is therefore intrinsic to the process.

## IN SUMMARY

Even after decades of designing and participating in learning labs, I continue to learn new ways for organizing and facilitating this important method of professional development. In this chapter, you have learned about different types of learning labs, you read through a variety of protocols, and you thought through some challenges related to facilitation.

There is plenty of evidence that shows that teachers believe that observations are well worth their time, but coaches still have to remain vigilant about making sure that the observations we facilitate are designed to move student learning forward. It isn't always easy for teachers to be out of the classroom, even for a half-day's observation, so we have to make that time count. It is also up to us to ensure that the teachers will receive support beyond the lab itself. The teachers at West High School understood how to make the observations count, because they were able to go into a colleague's classroom and learn a great deal . . . even on Cinco de Mayo.

# 8 Developing Systems to Prepare and Support Coaches

**M**any coaches will tell you that making the shift from teaching to coaching is dramatic. Coaches are often lonely and miss the close connections they had with students. Others are in roles that are poorly articulated. Some are not prepared for the complexities of working with adult learners. Others face school cultures that are downright hostile. To meet these challenges, coaches require support that is carefully designed to meet their unique needs.

This chapter will present both the *what* and the *how* for supporting coaches. The *what* refers to the curriculum or content that coaches need to succeed in their role. The *how* is the structure schools use to provide differentiated support to coaches. With both pieces in place, schools can offer just what coaches need.

## THE *WHAT*—A CURRICULUM FOR SUPPORTING COACHES

Like the seasons, coaches move through a series of predictable stages in their development. In the first few weeks of school, many are full of enthusiasm and hopefulness about the impact they will make on both the students and teachers. They are no longer constrained by the four walls of their classroom and instead are offered a broader sense of what's taking place within their school . . . a broader sense that has the potential to overwhelm and confuse many coaches. Coaches often worry that they, as individuals, won't have the time, energy, or knowledge to do what is required to move teacher and student learning forward.

Sure enough, just about when the leaves begin to fall, many coaches begin to feel discouraged about their work. They face the realization that their jobs are incredibly complex, that some teachers are hard to collaborate with, and that they simply may not have the direction they need to make the right decisions about their work. Understanding these seasons helps us design support for coaches that is timely and relevant (Figure 8.1).

## Support From the School Leader

I recently began working with Dulce, a principal in a large middle school in Florida. She was new to the district and was just becoming familiar with student-centered coaching.

Dulce didn't choose the coaches in her school; they had been hired by the previous administrator. Samantha was the math coach and Roxana the literacy coach. Since they were both new to coaching, Dulce wondered how well prepared they were for the job they were hired to do. They seemed to have a basic grasp of their role, but she wasn't sure how well they would assimilate into the school culture, engage teachers, create a schedule, and stay focused on the task at hand—increasing student performance. She suggested that since they all had a lot to learn about student-centered coaching, they'd figure it out together.

The pieces began to fall into place at a district meeting in mid-August. I had been hired to support the implementation of student-centered coaching, and we were kicking off the year with the principals and coaches. My goal was to generate a shared understanding of student-centered coaching across grades K–12 so that principals could become key players in supporting their team. There were over eighteen schools represented, and I knew that it might be my only opportunity to frame the coaching model in a way that would lead to implementation.

Many of the coaches were new to the role, and I expected that it would most likely be a difficult transition. They needed opportunities to collaborate with other coaches and receive individualized feedback about how they were doing. They also needed their principals to understand how to help them succeed. This raised the stakes for today's meeting, because I had to be sure that the principals understood the coaching practices deeply enough to provide ongoing feedback and support.

We began by identifying the core practices for student-centered coaching to establish a concrete vision for implementation. We discussed questions

**Figure 8.1** A Year at a Glance

|  | Common Challenges | Support |
|---|---|---|
| **Fall—August Through November** | Early in the year, new coaches are transitioning away from the classroom. They often worry about how to most effectively spend their time. Some receive little-to-no direction from the school leader about their work, making this stage in the year particularly stressful for coaches.<br><br>October is the toughest month for many new coaches as they gradually become more concerned regarding how to make an impact on student learning. | At this stage, coaches benefit from<br><br>• engaging in goal setting about their development as a coach,<br>• collaborating with the school leader about the coaching role,<br>• gaining techniques for fostering relationships with teachers,<br>• learning how to engage teachers in coaching cycles,<br>• designing a coaching schedule that makes the most impact on the students,<br>• incorporating tools to measure the impact of coaching on student learning,<br>• using strategies for facilitating small-group collaboration, and<br>• learning processes for using data and student work during coaching and collaboration. |
| **Winter— November Through February** | By now, most coaches have an established schedule that includes teachers who are the early adopters. Coaches recognize the need to develop strategies for gaining entry with teachers who have not yet engaged.<br><br>This is a great time for coaches to focus on coaching cycles before their work is interrupted by the spring testing season. | At this stage, coaches benefit from<br><br>• developing strategies for working with a broad range of adult learners,<br>• connecting with teachers, or teams of teachers, who haven't engaged in a coaching cycle,<br>• redesigning their schedule to accommodate teachers who are new to coaching, and<br>• continuing to refine coaching practices. |
| **Spring— March Through May** | The spring testing season arrives, and this often throws off the coach's schedule. While it is important to support testing, it shouldn't be all that a coach does. Even during this stage, coaching continues, and often the coach's best option is to work with departments that are least impacted by testing. | At this stage, coaches benefit from<br><br>• reflecting on the use of the Results-Based Coaching Tool (Figure 4.3) and how their coaching has impacted student learning and teaching practice across the year, and<br>• goal setting and planning for the next year. |

such as "What will the coaching look like in practice?" and "How will the coaches' time be spent?" After that, we unpacked each core practice to create a clear set of benchmarks for implementation (Figure 8.2). With a well-understood vision for coaching, the principals understood the expectations and could guide the coaching effort.

During a break, Dulce pulled me aside to share that the benchmarks had helped her understand student-centered coaching at a concrete level. She was getting a much better idea about what the coaches were expected to do and how to help them get there. Before now, student-centered coaching was just a concept she had heard of. Now, she had a clear vision for what it would be.

**Figure 8.2**   Benchmarks for Student-Centered Coaching

- Teachers have an established time to collaborate with the coach.
- Student work is analyzed during teacher collaboration.
- Teachers and the coach sort student work to plan differentiated instruction.
- Teachers and the coach co-plan, co-teach, and reflect on a regular basis.
- Formative assessments are used to identify the students' needs.
- Summative assessments are used to set schoolwide goals for improvement.
- There is flexibility in the pacing of instruction so that the students' needs are met.
- The questions used by the coach relate to student learning and instruction.
- Coaches document their impact on both student and teacher learning.
- The principal refrains from assigning coaching to teachers who are perceived to be struggling. This sends the message that coaching is for failing teachers and will undermine the model.
- The principal sets clear expectations so the staff knows what a coach is there to do and how coaching fits in with teacher evaluation.
- The principal spends time in classrooms and has a firm grasp on the effectiveness of the instruction throughout the school.

## Goal Setting

With the benchmarks in place, we provided the coaches and principals with some time to work together to set goals for the next few months. They created an action plan based on a rubric for student-centered coaching (Figure 8.8 in Tools and Techniques).

Both of the coaches in Dulce's school were skilled classroom teachers. Samantha was a teacher leader who had served on numerous math committees. Roxana was an experienced English teacher who had recently been studying literacy in the content areas. Both had participated in professional development around the Common Core Standards.

They had no trouble identifying goals based on the rubric. Samantha zeroed in on a goal to use student evidence in her coaching work. She knew a lot about formative assessment and thought that it was a good idea to be intentional about making the student work the centerpiece of her coaching conversations. She also knew that she had a tendency to come across as an expert and thought that using student work might help her steer clear of those behaviors.

Roxana was interested in learning more about facilitating small groups. She knew that the district expected her to lead professional learning communities (PLCs), and she was a bit anxious about this part of her work. She had heard nothing but moans and groans from the teachers about the PLCs and knew that she'd better be on her game to make sure the time was well spent.

After some discussion about their goals, the principals and coaches used an organizer to capture the action steps, checkpoints, and timeline for getting there (Figure 8.3). Creating the action plan provided the coaches with the opportunity to directly name what they would need from the school leader. The process established an open line of communication between the administrators and coaches and proved to be important for not only the new coaches but for the experienced coaches as well. It also ensured that when the principal became busy, the coach wouldn't fall through the cracks.

**Figure 8.3** Roxana's Goal-Setting Tool

| What skill would I like to develop as a coach? | What do I need to do to develop my skills? | How will I check in with the school leader about my progress? | What is the time line? |
|---|---|---|---|
| Develop ability to facilitate groups: I would like to ensure that PLCs are productive and student centered | Observe other coaches who are more experienced facilitators<br><br>Collect protocols and tools for facilitation<br><br>Begin using the protocols and tools with a group that I am comfortable with<br><br>Expand my work to other groups<br><br>Read professional books and articles on facilitation | Roxana will reflect with the principal about how she's doing with her action steps.<br><br>Dulce will observe Roxana as she facilitates a group.<br><br>Dulce will provide feedback to Roxana after she has observed Roxana facilitating a group.<br><br>As Roxana expands to facilitating more groups, Dulce will observe her a few more times. | Check in with Dulce on Week 2.<br><br>Dulce observes Roxana on Week 3.<br><br>Roxana expands to facilitating more groups by Week 5.<br><br>Dulce observes Roxana again on Week 6. |

# THE *HOW*—A FRAMEWORK FOR SUPPORTING COACHES

Mike Schmoker (2005) writes, "Isolation is the enemy of improvement" (p. 141), yet the isolation faced by coaches is hard to ignore. Most schools have a single coach on staff, two if they are lucky. And like teachers, coaches benefit from a framework of support that includes a variety of opportunities for collaboration.

Let's revisit the Three Venues of Professional Development from Chapter 6 as a helpful structure for designing a collaborative environment for coaches (Figure 8.4).

**Figure 8.4**  Three Venues of Professional Development—For Coaches

**Large Group**—Coaches meet as a district-level team to develop a shared understanding of the coaching model. At times, principals are included in these sessions to ensure the messages about coaching are clear and consistent throughout the system. Large-group sessions occur approximately two times each month and include coaches from different subject areas and grade levels.

**Small Group**—Coaches meet in small groups to refine their coaching practice, engage in facilitated observations, problem solve with colleagues, and work on subject or grade-level material. Providing time for smaller groups within the coaching cohort allows for a level of specificity that can't be reached in the large group. These sessions occur approximately two times each month and may take the form of team meetings or coaching observations.

**One-on-One**—District and school leaders provide coaches with individualized feedback to support their development. Feedback is linked directly to goal setting based on the Student-Centered Coaching Rubric (Figure 8.8).

# DIFFERENTIATING FOR COACHES

The needs of coaches inevitably vary. We often have to contend with high levels of turnover and differing levels of experience. The first year of implementation is relatively easy; we design the coaching model and then start implementing it. Then the second year arrives and inevitably there have been changes in personnel. Coaches who are new to the team haven't benefited from the learning of the previous year, and new principals aren't sure how to support the coaching model. At the same time, the rest of the team is ready to move forward with their learning. We obviously can't adopt a "learn on the job" mentality or the new coaches will surely suffer. But we also can't slow down the experienced members of the team or they'll feel as if their needs aren't being met either.

It is common practice for a district leader, such as an assistant superintendent, to be assigned as the point person responsible for supporting coaches. A problem with this approach rests in the fact that assistant superintendents have a lot on their plates. A typical day includes nonstop meetings at the district office and the tendency to be pulled in many different directions. It can be tremendously difficult for them to get out to the schools to meet with coaches at the level of frequency that coaches need to feel supported. It is for this reason that I suggest that principals serve as the primary source of support for coaches. They are on-site and tend to be equally as invested in moving the learning culture forward.

There will most likely be a learning curve for principals as they come to understand how to support the coaching effort. If they view coaching as silver bullet or a way to fix teachers, things will no doubt go awry. But if we can get principals and coaches on the same page about the core practices for coaching, then the support we offer to coaches will be differentiated and will occur more frequently.

In some districts, this is a no-brainer. District leaders expect principals to be a part of the conversation and are intentional about establishing a shared definition of coaching. In others, getting principals in the room is near-to-impossible. The rationale is that they are too busy to be pulled out of their schools for a meeting about coaching. This is a surefire way to create a failed coaching effort.

## ENGAGING RELUCTANT COACHES

Chapter 2 addressed the question of how to engage reluctant teachers. But the truth is, teachers aren't the only ones who might be reluctant. Coaches are often reluctant as well. I see them in every district I work with—coaches who are, as Jim Collins (2001) puts it, "Not on the right seat on the bus" (p. 41). Reluctant coaches present a myriad of challenges for both the school and district leadership. They are easy to spot because they are miserable. Coaching isn't easy, and you have to want to be there or you will be in for a very long school year.

Helping coaches feel confident about their work begins with a clearly articulated job description, and a clearly articulated job description begins with a clearly articulated set of performance indicators. What is the coach expected to achieve? What are the expected outcomes for coaching? How will performance be measured? The following section provides examples of how a district has grappled with issues around getting the right coaches on the team, evaluation of job performance, and creating opportunities for collaboration.

## A CASE IN POINT: SUPPORTING COACHES
## IN COUNCIL BLUFFS, IOWA

Evaluation can serve as a form of support. It makes clear the expectations for our day-to-day work and helps coaches understand the level of performance that is expected. Even so, I often come across districts that don't have any sort of evaluation tool for coaches, so they use a framework that was designed to evaluate teachers. This creates some obvious challenges for whoever is leading the coaching effort.

In the Council Bluffs Community School District, the contract required coaches to be evaluated using the same tool that is used for teachers. As a former coach himself, Corey Vorthmann, the supervisor of secondary education, knew that the coaches wouldn't get what they needed from the teacher evaluation, so he developed another way to provide them with feedback about their job performance.

Corey turned to the Student-Centered Coaching Rubric (Figure 8.8) to provide a clear set of performance indicators that he could put in the hands of the coaches and principals. He felt that the rubric offered clarity about what the coaches should be doing and, in turn, clearly identified the support that they would need.

The rubric also helped Corey make decisions about who would be a good fit for the coaching team. He understood that it was unlikely that he would find candidates who were skilled in every area on the rubric, so he had to think carefully about which skills would be the easiest to grow and which skills he would expect the coaches to have from the get-go. He knew that while he could build a coach's skill set, it would be quite difficult to shift their beliefs and philosophy about how students learn. He needed people on his team with a growth mindset and the stance of a learner. He also needed people who believed in students and understood how to design instruction to move their learning forward. He used the rubric as a tool to hone the hiring process to address the following questions:

- Does the candidate have a well-developed understanding of best practices?
- Does the candidate have a proven track record as a classroom teacher?
- Has the candidate ever participated in coaching?
- Is the candidate willing to work in unfamiliar content areas?
- Would the candidate be best described as a learner, an expert, or both?
- Does the candidate believe that all students can succeed?
- What are some coaching practices that the candidate would like to develop?

*(Continued)*

(Continued)

## Coaching Labs in Council Bluffs

In Council Bluffs, coaching labs were an indispensable tool for providing needs-based and differentiated support to the coaches. Chapter 7 introduced learning labs for teachers, and in *Learning Along the Way* (2003), I expanded the model to include coaching labs as well.

> Coaching labs provide coaches with the opportunity to meet with a small group of colleagues and observe a fellow coach who acts as a lab host. The goal of the labs is to provide coaches with time to observe one another's practice, as well as time for rigorous reflection. Participating coaches walk away with new ideas and tools for their own work and are able to take time in their busy professional lives to reflect. (p. 38)

The coaching lab that featured Joel and the coaches from Wilson Middle School in Chapter 5 included all of the secondary principals, assistant principals, and coaches from the district. We brought them together to develop an understanding about how coaches and principals can collaborate in a way that makes strategic use of the coaches and results in increased student performance.

On the day of the observation, we gathered in a horseshoe and scripted the conversation between Joel and the coaches. After the observation, we engaged in a debriefing session that was designed to peel back the layers of what was observed. Our desired outcome was for the coaches and principals to reflect on what they observed and consider how it might impact the way they were collaborating with their own coach.

While that observation included school leaders, other coaching labs in Council Bluffs have included the coaching team and have focused on different aspects of their role:

- Planning sessions with a teacher or team of teachers
- Planning sessions with the principal
- Small-group collaboration or PLCs
- Co-teaching or modeling in the classroom
- Observing a teacher to provide feedback

## Questioning During Coaching Labs

While Corey believes that coaching labs are a beneficial form of support for his team, he continually works to refine how to get the most out of the observations. He doesn't want the labs to just scratch the surface or create superficial conversations. Instead, his intention is for the labs to take the participants' thinking to a deeply reflective place. He doesn't want labs to be about getting ideas—that is easy to accomplish. Instead, his goal is to help the participants uncover the meaning behind what was observed and apply it to their own work.

Coaches at all experience levels are encouraged to host a coaching lab. To plan the observation, Corey meets with the lab host to frame an overarching question that is rooted in the coach's plan for professional growth. Typically, the question comes from an area where the coach feels stuck and needs support from a group of peers. It can take a fair amount of conversation to land on a question that is both authentic and rigorous enough to frame a coaching lab. Figure 8.5 provides some sample focus questions for coaching labs that Corey and I have facilitated.

**Figure 8.5**  Sample Focus Questions From Coaching Labs

- As a coach, how can I build teachers' skills in analyzing student work?
- During PLCs, how can I encourage teachers to question one another in ways that promote student learning?
- When meeting with the principal, how can I encourage specificity around what the teachers should or should not be doing in their classrooms?
- How can I *decrease* my input in conversations in order to *increase* the input that is provided by others?
- What are some strategies for holding teachers accountable for doing what they say they will do?

In addition to the focus question, lab participants are expected to generate their own questions during the lab process. We have noticed that there is a learning curve when it comes to generating the questions that take the conversation deep. It can be helpful for observers to think carefully about the purpose for their question. Is it about clarifying what they are seeing? Gathering information? Or is the purpose to better understand what they observed?

Participants can also consider the level of the question based on Bloom's Taxonomy. Is it a lower-level question that is geared toward gathering knowledge or information? Or would it be considered a higher-level question that is about application, analysis, synthesis, or evaluation? We are after high-level questions during coaching labs, because those questions help the observers understand what they are observing and apply what they are seeing to their own work.

We designed the following tool to refine the team's questioning skills. In the left-hand column, the coaches record their questions. In the middle column, they identify why they are asking the question. And in the right-hand column, they consider the level of the question. We don't intend to use this

*(Continued)*

(Continued)

tool during every coaching lab. Instead, we expect that by inserting some practice into the art of questioning, future labs will become more rigorous and reflective (Figure 8.6).

**Figure 8.6**  Developing Questioning Skills

| Question | Purpose | Bloom's Taxonomy— Level of Depth <br> Circle one: |
|---|---|---|
| How can I build data into more of my coaching conversations? | I am trying to apply what I observed to my own coaching conversations. | Knowledge <br> Comprehension <br> (Application) <br> Analysis <br> Synthesis <br> Evaluation |
| How do you feel about where the students ended up at the end of the instructional block? | I am seeking to understand the impact that was made on the students during the observation. | Knowledge <br> Comprehension <br> Application <br> (Analysis) <br> Synthesis <br> Evaluation |

## Collecting Student Evidence

In addition to asking thoughtful questions, a skillful observer has to be able to capture and share evidence that is specific and focused. I have participated in hundreds of learning labs, and I still struggle with a productive way to capture what I see in my notes in a way that provides me with the necessary level of detail. I would love to be able to capture every word and I usually try to do so, but the conversation inevitably moves faster than I can transcribe, and whether I'm using a laptop or notepad, I always struggle to keep up.

The quality of the notes that the observers take drives the quality of the debriefing session. The goal is specificity and depth, and that's hard to attain without a full record of the conversation. Here are some notes I took during a portion of a coaching lab in Council Bluffs. We observed Rob, a coach, in a planning conversation with a math teacher named Imad. You'll notice that it is essentially a script of the conversation. I also added in a few questions along the way. By scripting to this level of detail, I have a lot to share during the debriefing session (Figure 8.7).

---

**Figure 8.7**  Sample Notes From a Coaching Lab

| | |
|---|---|
| **Rob:** | My thinking is that today, we will create a plan for student learning. What would the student work look like in a perfect world? |
| **Imad:** | They should solve the problems and complete the projects. We can test that by the formal assessments, quizzes, and tests. I also like to do discussions, so I know who understands it and who doesn't. |
| **Rob:** | How can you tell when one student understands and another doesn't? |
| **Imad:** | By the reasoning that the students use. I can also tell what they are talking about by how they solve the problem and how they approach the problem. |
| **Rob:** | How are you collecting evidence about how the students approach the problem? |
| **Imad:** | I'm doing one problem with the calculator and one without the calculator. |
| **Rob:** | Do you have some student evidence that shows how the students are doing? Would you mind sorting through those right now? |

*Imad goes to get the student work.*

| | |
|---|---|
| **Rob:** | Before we figure out how to sort these, what would a perfect one look like? |

*Imad points to an example.*

*Question—How will Rob identify the learning targets with Imad?*

---

## TOOLS AND TECHNIQUES

### Student-Centered Coaching Rubric

The following rubric details the skills that the coach and school leader need to design a model of coaching that impacts student learning. It can be used to design a system of support for coaches and principals, to complete individualized goal setting, and even to formally evaluate a coach or coaching effort (Figure 8.8).

### Coaching Lab Protocol

A while back, I led a project that included coaching labs across the Denver Public Schools. I knew we had to create a skilled team of facilitators

**Figure 8.8** Student-Centered Coaching Rubric

| Trait: Understands and Implements Student-Centered Coaching | | | |
|---|---|---|---|
| | **Accomplished** | **Developing** | **Novice** |
| **The Coach** | Student evidence directly and consistently informs coaching conversations. The coach seamlessly guides the conversation from student learning to other factors, such as the implementation of a program or curriculum and classroom routines. | The coach is beginning to draw on student evidence in coaching sessions. The coach is more capable in addressing other factors, such as the implementation of a program or curriculum and classroom routines, in the context of student learning. | The coach rarely draws from student evidence in coaching sessions. Coaching is wholly focused on teaching practice, implementation of a program or curriculum, or classroom routines. |
| **The School Leader** | The principal understands the core practices for student-centered coaching, subscribes to those practices, and provides support to move the coach's work forward.<br><br>The principal provides the necessary pressure and support to the adult learners in the school. | The principal has some knowledge of the core practices for student-centered coaching or may question its value.<br><br>The principal is beginning to find a balance between providing adequate pressure and support to the adult learners in the school. | The principal is not supportive of or lacks knowledge in the core practices for student-centered coaching.<br><br>The principal has not yet achieved a balance of providing pressure and support to the adult learners in the school. |
| **Trait: Understands How to Work With Adult Learners** | | | |
| **The Coach** | The coach has a well-formed understanding of adult learners and flexibly adapts the coaching based on this knowledge to move the adult learning forward. | The coach has taken specific measures to develop an understanding of adult learners. The coach is more able to pinpoint and remedy problems when working with teachers. | The coach has little knowledge of adult learners and has a hard time pinpointing the cause of problems when working with teachers. |
| **The School Leader** | The principal understands adult learners and creates a safe environment in which adults can take risks as learners. | The principal is growing more adaptable to the adult learners in the school. There is more evidence of teachers taking risks as learners. | The principal takes a passive approach or mandates change and expects the coach to hold teachers accountable to implement the change. |

| | Accomplished | Developing | Novice |
|---|---|---|---|
| | The principal has established a clear vision and teachers understand what is expected of them. | The principal is honing the school vision and is more comfortable holding teachers accountable for certain practices. | There is confusion among teachers regarding what is expected of them. |
| **Trait: Knowledge of Effective Teaching Practices and Standards** | | | |
| **The Coach** | The coach has extensive experience in a broad range of levels and subjects. The coach continues to broaden his or her experience in order to deepen the current knowledge base of the standards. | The coach has taken specific measures to broaden the range of teaching experience across a range of levels and subjects. The coach is currently developing knowledge of the content and standards that are being coached. | The coach is capable and experienced across a limited range of levels and subjects. The coach is still gaining experience in the content and standards that are being coached. |
| **The School Leader** | The school leader has a well-developed pedagogical understanding and is able to recognize and provide feedback to teachers in direct relationship to the expected teaching practices. | The school leader has a developing sense of pedagogy and may understand some areas of instruction better than others. The school leader is able to provide specific feedback in some areas, but not all. | The school leader lacks pedagogical understanding and is therefore unable to provide teachers with specific expectations and feedback regarding instruction. |
| **Trait: Builds Relationships** | | | |
| **The Coach** | The coach works effectively with all teachers due to specific measures that were taken to build trusting and professional relationships. | The coach is beginning to build trusting relationships with a broader array of teachers, including more challenging teachers. | The coach is able to build trusting relationships with a limited group of teachers. |
| **The School Leader** | The school leader works effectively to build collegial relationships with teachers and also understands the importance of providing the coach with the time | The school leader is working toward the development of collegial relationships with teachers but struggles to provide the coach with the necessary support to build and sustain collegial | The school leader questions the role of relationships and collegiality in the school setting or may struggle personally to build collegial |

*(Continued)*

**Figure 8.8** (Continued)

|  | Accomplished | Developing | Novice |
|---|---|---|---|
|  | that it takes to build and sustain collegial relationships. | relationships with teachers. | relationships with teachers. |
| **Trait: Skilled Facilitation** | | | |
| **The Coach** | The coach understands which facilitation processes to employ at any given time. The coach is a skilled facilitator, and as a result, both small and large groups function in a highly productive manner on a consistent basis. | The coach is working to expand the repertoire of facilitation techniques used in small- and large-group sessions. Groups are beginning to function in a more productive level. | The coach employs a limited set of facilitation processes. Small- and/or large-group facilitation is not productive on a consistent basis. |
| **The School Leader** | The school leader also understands and employs facilitation processes that support group work. | The school leader is working to develop the necessary skills to support group work through facilitative processes. | The school leader is unclear regarding the skills related to leading group work. |
| **Trait: Maintains a Learning Stance** | | | |
| **The Coach** | The coach consistently seeks new experiences and opportunities for learning rather than taking the stance of an expert. | The coach takes advantage of some opportunities for new learning and is becoming more comfortable taking the stance of co-learner with teachers. | The coach does not take advantage of opportunities for new learning on a consistent basis and does not take the stance of a co-learner with teachers. |
| **The School Leader** | The school leader sets the tone that "we are all learners" and models this behavior as an individual. | The school leader is working toward developing transparency regarding his or her learning and development. | The school leader reinforces the status quo rather than establishing a learning environment. |
| **Trait: Reflective Dialogue** | | | |
| **The Coach** | The coach encourages reflective dialogue by asking open-ended questions, probing, and | The coach is beginning to use strategies such as asking open-ended questions, probing, and | The coach does not use conversational approaches that encourage reflective |

| | Accomplished | Developing | Novice |
|---|---|---|---|
| | paraphrasing techniques rather than simply giving the teacher answers. | paraphrasing techniques to encourage reflective dialogue among teachers. | dialogue among teachers. |
| **The School Leader** | The school leader uses specific strategies to encourage reflective dialogue among teachers. | The school leader is working toward the development of a reflective school culture. | The school leader is beginning to develop strategies for encouraging teacher reflection. |
| **Trait: Productive Relationship Between the Coach and School Leader** | | | |
| **The Coach** | The coach understands his or her appropriate role as a coach while also understanding how to work collaboratively with the school leader. | The coach and school leader are beginning to find better definitions regarding their unique roles and are beginning to collaborate. | The coach and school leader do not work collaboratively. The coach is unclear regarding the coaching role and how it relates to the role of the school leader. |
| **The School Leader** | The school leader fully understands and supports the implementation of student-centered coaching.<br><br>Time is allocated for the school leader to provide the coach with feedback based on his or her goals. | The school leader is developing an understanding of student-centered coaching. The principal and coach meet informally to touch base, but feedback to the coach is less predictable and inconsistent. | The school leader is developing an understanding of student-centered coaching. The principal and coach do not meet together or work collaboratively. |

for the observations and that I had to be absolutely certain that no coaches who were observed would be scarred by the experience.

At our first session with a new team of facilitators, we heard from a panel of coaches who had previously participated in coaching labs. We asked the panelists what advice they had for anyone who would be facilitating a coaching lab. Over and over they said, "Use a protocol." I couldn't have agreed more. Without a protocol, it is hard to predict in what direction the conversation will go. With a protocol, coaches feel secure and know that they won't be thrown under the bus.

The following protocol moves the conversation through series of rounds that are designed to capture a rich combination of evidence of what was observed and the implications for student and teacher learning. Feel free to adapt it to suit your needs, but by all means, listen to the coaches and use a protocol (Figure 8.9).

**Figure 8.9** Coaching Lab Protocol

**Prebrief**

The host of the coaching lab provides the context and focus for the observation. Typically, the observation is framed around a dilemma that needs to be solved or a goal that the coach or principal are working toward. By framing the observation around a dilemma or goal, the host provides the observers with the opportunity to support their colleague and also to reflect on their own work with teachers.

**Observation**

The group observes a coaching conversation as it happens. While observing, participants take notes that will inform the debriefing session. Often, coaching labs focus on one of the following areas:

- Planning sessions with a teacher or team of teachers
- Planning sessions with the principal
- Small-group collaboration or PLCs
- Co-teaching or modeling in the classroom
- Observing a teacher to provide feedback

**Debrief**

The debriefing session is guided by the following rounds. A whip-around format is used so that each observer has a turn to share. At the end of each round, the facilitator synthesizes the key points from the round. The lab host listens and takes notes in order to respond during the fourth round.

*Round 1: Coaching Observations*

- What did you see, notice, or hear during the coaching conversation?

*Round 2: Connection to Student Learning*

- How will student learning be influenced by the coaching conversation?

*Round 3: Questions*

- What questions do you have for the lab host?

*Round 4: Lab Host Responds*

- How would the lab host like to respond to what was shared?

*Round 5: Group Reflection and Next Steps*

- What were the implications of what you observed? What is your next step for your work with teachers?

## Coaching Portfolio: A Year in Review

Helping coaches reflect on their work is an essential part of their growth. In the St. Joseph School District, we created a coaching portfolio in which the coaches were asked to reflect upon and document the impact they made on both teacher and student learning (Figure 8.10).

**Figure 8.10** Coaching Portfolio

**Documentation of Impact**

- Provide a Results-Based Coaching Tool for each team and/or individual you worked with in a coaching cycle. (See Chapter 4 for more on the Results-Based Coaching Tool.)
- Include any other tools you have used to document your coaching impact (i.e., teacher surveys, collaborative review of student work, post-cycle conferences, etc.).

**Summary of Goals**

- List all of the goals you set for yourself this year.
- Explain where you've shown the most growth and why.
- Explain the goals you are still working toward achieving and why.

**Three Venues of Professional Development**

- In which venues have you spent most of your time as a coach? Why?
- Where do you plan to focus next year? Why?

**Final Reflections**

- What did you learn about your coaching as you went through this process?
- What are your next steps for continuing to develop as a coach?

## IN SUMMARY

We can't get around the fact that coaches are their own islands, living in a no-man's-land between the teachers and administration. But that doesn't mean that we can't throw out a life preserver now and then.

Supporting a team of coaches isn't easy. It demands a vision that meets the requirements of both the individual and the system. While the system moves toward a certain goal or objective, our coaches are doing the same thing.

Having a clear sense of what we are expected to accomplish is important. Providing coaches with a rubric or criteria about their work is a step in that direction. Coaches also need to set goals in relationship to the criteria. We all feel better when we are moving forward in developing our own expertise. Even so, setting goals means very little without the necessary feedback and support to achieve those goals. Ongoing conversations and feedback from the school and district leaders provides coaches with the direction they need to achieve success. Coaches no longer have to feel alone. They can be a part of a system that provides targeted support that matches their unique needs.

# In Closing

It isn't unusual for those of us living in Colorado to come up with all kinds of crazy ways to push ourselves to the limit. Hundred-mile mountain bike races, ultramarathons, and other extreme activities are disturbingly commonplace. It's from this crowd that I learned about the *fun scale*. To most of us more mortal souls, it may be seen as a justification for doing crazy things. But for people who like to push themselves, it's a reality.

I learned about the fun scale from my friend Craig, an amputee and world-champion rock climber. He referred to a recent five-day, record-breaking climb of El Capitan as *Type 2 fun*. I had to know how he could possibly use the word *fun* to describe the experience. It turns out that in his crowd of outdoor enthusiasts, they like to rate everything, even fun. With a completely straight face, he walked me through the fun scale: *Type 1 fun* is just plain fun—enjoyable while it's happening. It really doesn't take a lot of work or effort. Sitting on a beach at sunset is what I'd call Type 1 fun.

*Type 2 fun* is more intense. You may wonder why you signed up for it, and you may even try to escape to that beach at sunset. What makes Type 2 fun worth it is it feels really good afterward. When I am coaching, I'm having Type 2 fun. While I'm not physically exhausted, as I would be if I were climbing El Capitan, I am so engaged in what I'm doing that I walk away feeling an enormous sense of accomplishment. I think that's why I love it so much. I find myself happiest when I am having Type 2 fun, and I suspect that this is true for many educators. After all, we went into this professional to make a difference and serve others—not something I'd characterize as *easy*.

Then there's *Type 3 fun*. Type 3 fun isn't fun at all. It's such a challenge that there is simply not a lot of payoff. Climbing Mount Everest could be described (for most of us) as Type 3 fun. I sometimes meet coaches who feel like they are climbing Mount Everest. This makes me sad and leads me to wonder if coaching is the right fit. Coaches have to embrace the challenges that are intrinsic to their work, but they shouldn't be miserable.

The landscape in education is changing at a rapid pace. Twenty years ago, I began teaching in a system that is not recognizable today. There were no standards, no such thing as formative assessments, teachers rarely collaborated, and there were no established best practices for teaching and learning. We operated based on our personal style or on what our gut told us to do for our students.

A lot has changed, thanks to the work of educators such as Linda Darling-Hammond, Rick DuFour, Grant Wiggins, and Jay McTighe. Today, educators have become quite used to discussing how to best serve their students. Schools are more collaborative, and we have time and resources that didn't exist in the past. We finally have what we need for coaching to thrive.

Implementing student-centered coaching boils down to the belief that if we focus on student learning, we can improve the quality of the teaching as well. Since coaching has traditionally been teacher centered, this change of mindset may be a significant paradigm shift to some.

Pairing this shift in mindset with the core practices that have been introduced in this book will help coaches get the results they are hoping for. From there, it's simply about trusting the process and embracing the fact that our work is complex and interesting. Each scenario is unique. Each conversation is framed around the needs of a distinct group of students. Our work has meaning. It is most definitely Type 2 fun.

# Resources to Support Student-Centered Coaching

## Websites

ASCD—www.ascd.org

Choice Literacy—www.choiceliteracy.com

Diane Sweeney Consulting—www.dianesweeney.com

Educational Leadership—www.ascd.org/publications/educationalleadership.aspx

Learning Forward—www.learningforward.org

Literacy Coaching Clearinghouse—www.literacycoachingonline.org

## Books and Articles

Bambrick-Santoyo, P. (2010). *Driven by data*. San Francisco, CA: Jossey-Bass.

Barth, R. (2006, March). Improving relationships in the schoolhouse. *Educational Leadership*, pp. 8–13.

Bean, R., & DeFord, D. (2007). *Do's and don'ts for literacy coaching*. Retrieved from www.literacycoachingonline.org/briefs/DosandDontsFinal.pdf

Burkins, J. M. (2007). *Coaching for balance: How to meet the challenges of literacy coaching*. Newark, DE: International Reading Association.

DuFour, R., Eaker, R., & DuFour, R. (2005). *On common ground: The power of professional learning communities*. Bloomington, IN: NES.

Evans, R. (1996). *The human side of school change: Reform, resistance, and the real-life problems of innovation*. San Francisco, CA: Jossey-Bass.

Flaherty, J. (1999). *Coaching: Evoking excellence in others*. Boston, MA: Butterworth-Heinemann.

Frost, S., Buhle, R., & Blachowicz, C. (2009). *Effective literacy coaching: Building expertise and a culture of literacy.* Alexandria, VA: ASCD.

Fullan, M. (2001). *Leading in a culture of change.* San Francisco, CA: Jossey-Bass.

Fullan, M. (2006). *Change theory: A force for school improvement.* Retrieved from www.michaelfullan.com/media/13396072630.pdf

Killion, J., & Harrison, C. (2006). *Taking the lead: New roles for teachers and school-based coaches.* Oxford, OH: NSDC.

Knight, J. (2007). *Instructional coaching: A partnership approach to improving instruction.* Thousand Oaks, CA: Corwin.

Knight, J. (2009). *Coaching: Approaches and perspectives.* Thousand Oaks, CA: Corwin.

Lencioni, P. (2002). *The five dysfunctions of a team.* San Francisco, CA: Jossey-Bass.

Lovely, S., & Buffum, A. (2005). *Generations at school.* Thousand Oaks, CA: Corwin.

Marshall, K. (2009). *Rethinking teacher supervision and evaluation.* San Francisco, CA: Jossey-Bass.

Muhammad, A. (2009). *Transforming school culture.* Bloomington, IN: Solution Tree Press.

Rader, H. (2012). *Side by side: Short takes on best practice for teachers and literacy leaders.* Holden, ME: Choice Literacy.

Sadder, M., & Nidus, G. (2009). *The literacy coach's game plan.* Newark, DE: International Reading Association.

Schlechty, P. (2011). *Engaging students: The next level of working on the work.* San Francisco, CA: Jossey-Bass.

Sweeney, D. (2010). *Student-centered coaching: A guide for K–8 coaches and principals.* Thousand Oaks, CA: Corwin.

Toll, C. (2005). *The literacy coach's survival guide.* Newark, DE: International Reading Association.

Wheatley, M. J. (2002). *Turning to one another: Simple conversations to restore hope to the future.* San Francisco, CA: Berrett-Koehler Publishers.

Wiggins, G., & McTighe, J. (2005). *Understanding by design.* Alexandria, VA: ASCD.

# References

Bambrick-Santoyo, P. (2010). *Driven by data: A practical guide to improve instruction.* San Francisco, CA: Jossey-Bass.

Barth, R. (2007). *Educational leadership.* San Francisco, CA: Jossey-Bass.

Black, P., & Wiliam, D. (1998). Inside the black box: Raising standards through classroom assessment. *Phi Delta Kappan, 80*(2), 139–144.

Burkins, J. M. (2007). *Coaching for balance: How to meet the challenges of literacy coaching.* Newark, DE: International Reading Association.

Collins, J. (2001). *Good to great.* New York, NY: HarperCollins.

DuFour, R., Eaker, R., & DuFour, R. (2005). *On common ground: The power of professional learning communities.* Bloomington, IN: Solution Tree Press.

Flaherty, J. (1999). *Coaching: Evoking excellence in others.* Boston, MA: Butterworth-Heinemann.

Fullan, M. (2009). *The challenge of change.* Thousand Oaks, CA: Corwin.

Hattie, J. (2009). *Visible learning: A synthesis of over 800 meta-analyses relating to achievement.* Auckland, New Zealand: Routledge.

Jensen, E. (2009). *Teaching with poverty in mind.* Alexandria, VA: ASCD.

Killion, J., & Harrison, C. (2006). *Taking the lead: New roles for teachers and school-based coaches.* Oxford, OH: NSDC.

Knight, J. (2007). *Instructional coaching: A partnership approach to improving instruction.* Thousand Oaks, CA: Corwin.

Lemov, D. (2010). *Teach like a champion: 49 techniques that put students on the path to college.* San Francisco, CA: Jossey-Bass.

Marshall, K. (2009). *Rethinking teacher supervision and evaluation.* San Francisco, CA: Jossey-Bass.

Marzano, R., Pickering, D., & Pollack, J. (2012). *Classroom instruction that works, 2nd edition.* Alexandria, VA: ASCD.

Muhammad, A. (2009). *Transforming school culture: How to overcome staff division.* Bloomington, IN: Solution Tree Press.

National Governors Association Center for Best Practices, Council of Chief State School Officers. (2010). *Common Core State Standards.* Washington, DC.

Schein, E. (1994). *Organizational culture and leadership.* San Francisco, CA: Jossey-Bass.

Schmoker, M. (2005). *On common ground.* Bloomington, IN: Solution Tree Press.

Stiggins, R., Arter, J., Chappuis, J., & Chappuis, S. (2006). *Classroom assessment for student learning: Doing it right, using it well.* Princeton, NJ: ETS.

Stone, D., Patton, B., & Heen, S. (2010). *Difficult conversations: How to discuss what matters most.* New York, NY: Penguin.

Sweeney, D. (2003). *Learning along the way: Professional development by and for teachers.* Portland, ME: Stenhouse.

Tomlinson, C. A., & McTighe, J. (2006). *Integrating differentiated instruction and understanding by design.* Alexandria, VA: ASCD.

Tovani, C. (2011). *So what do they really know?* Portland, ME: Stenhouse.

Wiggins, G., & McTighe, J. (2005). *Understanding by design, 2nd edition.* Alexandria, VA: ASCD.

# Index

# CORWIN

A SAGE Company

The Corwin logo—a raven striding across an open book—represents the union of courage and learning. Corwin is committed to improving education for all learners by publishing books and other professional development resources for those serving the field of PreK–12 education. By providing practical, hands-on materials, Corwin continues to carry out the promise of its motto: **"Helping Educators Do Their Work Better."**